NEW EYES FOR OLD

NEW EYES FOR OLD:
NONFICTION WRITINGS BY RICHARD McKENNA

∾ Selected and edited by
EVA GRICE McKENNA &
SHIRLEY GRAVES COCHRANE

JOHN F. BLAIR, *Publisher*
Winston-Salem, North Carolina

Acknowledgments

THE editors wish to express their appreciation to the following publishers in whose pages some of the speeches and articles included in the present volume have previously appeared: *The Texas Quarterly* for permission to reprint "New Eyes for Old"; *North Carolina Libraries* for permission to reprint "Adventures with Libraries"; the Raleigh *News and Observer* for permission to reprint parts of "The Wreck of Uncle Josephus"; *The Rebel*, East Carolina University, for permission to reprint "On Creative Energy"; *The Writer* for permission to reprint "On Becoming a Writer," there published as "Creative Energy and Fiction Writing"; *The Texas Quarterly* for permission to reprint "Journey with a Little Man"; also Harper & Row, Publishers, Inc., for permission to reprint "Journey with a Little Man" from *The Sons of Martha and Other Stories* by Richard McKenna. Copyright © 1964 by Eva McKenna. By permission of Harper & Row, Publishers, Inc.

Contents

Editorial Note

⮌ WHEN Richard McKenna died suddenly in November, 1964, he had written the best-selling novel, *The Sand Pebbles*, a dozen or so short stories, and one-third of the first draft of a second novel. The unfinished novel had within it three episodes that were distinct entities, and these, together with some shorter fiction, were published under the title the author had selected for his novel: *The Sons of Martha* (Harper & Row Publishers, Inc., 1967).

But a consideration of McKenna's literary legacy is not complete without due attention to his nonfiction writings. In the time span between the publication of *The Sand Pebbles* and the isolation he required to write *The Sons of Martha*, he had delivered nearly a dozen speeches, all enthusiastically received. He spoke on subjects ranging from education to the writing process, with a strong uniting theme of Man's capacity for growth and accomplishment. The speeches combined wit, style, fancy, and imagination with solid learning in both the sciences and the humanities.

The present volume includes most of these speeches, together with an article originally appearing in *The Writer*. For all their readability and ease of communication they represent a serious effort on McKenna's part to formulate his theories of education and to state his literary aesthetic.

With the publication of these nonfiction writings, Richard McKenna's work and thought are more fully represented than with his fiction alone. The editors feel that the book also compensates in some small measure for the untimely end to his writing career.

S.G.C.

❧ PART I

Obtaining an Education

From a speech before the University of North Carolina Faculty Club, Chapel Hill, N. C., December 11, 1962

New Eyes for Old:
The Quest for Education

‸WHEN I began to marshal my thoughts on the subject of the quest for education, they were neither as many nor as sure of themselves as I had hoped they might be. A bit of wisdom I have learned came to my aid. I did not get anywhere in writing until I learned to write only of matters which I knew about from direct personal experience. So I will limit my remarks to my own quest for education and the great part played in it by the University of North Carolina. That has the added virtue of reducing the complexity of the subject by a factor of about three billion, or whatever the population of the Earth was at the last estimate.

For most of my life the word *education* has, to me, meant *book learning*. I understand well enough now the notion of character-formation contained in the word. But I must understand also that not one of the billions of people whom I am conveniently leaving out of this discussion has reached or will reach maturity without gaining that kind of education, no matter how deficient he may be in book learning. His whole society is his teacher, and no one can play hooky from that school. Of course there is much talk about good and bad character. I am not competent to tread among those razor blades. A few years ago I was puzzled by the public dismay over the TV quiz scandals. I had not known until then that much book learning was supposed to be coupled with greater moral worth.

In my own formative years I never encountered the equivalent of Mark Hopkins; I know him best even now as a tall, glass-headed structure in San Francisco within which almost anything

might happen.* Yet the other end of my log was by no means untenanted. Lumberjacks and miners, old cowboys and Indian fighters, Basque sheepherders and Mexican section hands all sat there. As a boy I was drawn to old men and to men of exotic origins. Later there were old sailors and beachcombers of a dozen nationalities and many Japanese and Chinese in Far Eastern seaports. I have forgotten most of their names. No single one of them stays in my memory as a tremendously impressive individual. Yet I am convinced that in their aggregate they would outweigh Mark Hopkins. I think men's characters are formed more by their casual daily encounters with other ordinary people, as ball bearings are brought to perfect sphericity by randomly tumbling against each other in a barrel, than by any skilled institutional machine work.

No man has to go questing after a moral education. Some kind of moral education, and commonly the most useful kind, is going to be unavoidably thrust upon him. In a course in anthropology here I was pleased and amused to learn the distinction anthropologists make between the overt and the covert value-systems of a culture. Their methodology is much older than the science which uses it. First they ask a representative sample of the people what they would do in various hypothetical situations involving choice, and they make notes of the answers. Then, saying nothing, they observe what the people actually do when they are confronted with similar real situations, and they make a different set of notes. I think in our own culture that kind of anthropological fieldwork is perforce begun by every child at about the age of five. When he reaches a point, if ever, where he can be once more unconscious of the discrepancy, his moral education may be said to be complete. In so far as our society has institutionalized means of anesthetizing the pain caused by the split in our moral

*Mr. McKenna was under a misapprehension. The Mark Hopkins Hotel in San Francisco was named for Mark Hopkins, the railroad financier, rather than Mark Hopkins, the educator.

personality, perhaps one might after all speak of a quest for moral education. Since I never undertook that quest, I must disqualify myself from further remarks upon it. I will talk only about book learning.

My early book learning came to me as naturally as the season in the public school of the little town in which I grew up. I did well, but I think I studied primarily only to please my teachers. I seemed able to appease my curiosity about the nature of things simply by looking at the world around me without much discrimination. Quite early I began to find a special charm in an unpeopled world, the waste of lava rock and sagebrush desert surrounding my home. I was much alone in that desert, and I never felt lonely. I was often more purely happy at such times than I think I have ever been since.

For many years I felt obliged to think ill of myself and hold those memories a guilty pleasure. Then I met Thoreau, and later, here at the University, I met William Wordsworth, and I have been relieved of that small pain.

When I was a very young man, I went to China as a United States sailor. I had no very keen regrets that my education, in the sense of supervised book learning, had ended. My modest store was still greater than that of most of the men among whom I lived. I was busy learning military life and steam engineering without the mediation of books. I learned how to be alone on a ship at sea simply by leaning on the rail and looking out to the horizon. The sea yielded me the same curious pleasure that the desert had. I found that I could wander the streets and temple courtyards of Oriental cities much as I had once lingered in the desert. A screen of strangeness stood between me and the busy human living I observed. I could be tolerated as observer without being compelled to participate. It seemed to me that I could and often did participate in the lives of those about me with the same strange sympathy I knew how to feel toward forms in the desert. They would feel it too. Without a word of language in common,

possibly by virtue of that, we could often exchange smiles or join in laughter or make a little game with children. No human interaction has ever seemed more real to me.

That was education, but it was not book learning. In connection with book learning, I want to recount just one memory of that other sort. It is a memory that often forced itself to my attention in the years when I was learning that I would have to attend a university.

There was a little bar, run by a Japanese man and his wife, in the Wanchai district of Hong Kong. It had only two tables and six or eight chairs, and it was clean and neat and orderly beyond the average of such places. I never saw anything really rowdy go on there. The unique feature of the place was a large wire cage on a shelf at one side of the room. In the cage were four white rats.

The rats were the entertainers. They were lean and hollow of flank, and their eyes were a fierce red. They would prowl the straw litter in the bottom of their cage and from eyes red with hatred they would watch the sailors drinking beer at the tables. When a customer passed near their cage, they would press against the bars, squeaking faintly and hoping to get a nip at him.

The sailors relished the helpless hatred of the rats. Often a man would tease them with a finger through the bars. The rats would fly around inside their cage almost like birds, in a great squeaking rage, trying to catch the teasing finger. If the man kept it up long enough, one of the rats would usually catch his finger. Then we would all laugh while the mamasan came to unclamp the rat's jaws. The rats would not bite the mamasan.

When closing time was near, around midnight, the mamasan would put an egg into the cage. I think the rats were deliberately kept starved, because I never saw any water or any other food go into the cage. The egg made the best show of all. Instantly the rats would be at it. They knew there was food inside it. But they were not able to break the egg. They would bite at it, but they could not open their jaws wide enough to get a purchase with

their teeth. Their teeth would just slide off. They would all be frantic to get at it at once. The egg would disappear inside what looked like a white ball of interwoven rats. The ball of rats would roll slowly around the floor of the cage, with a constant muffled squeaking and a constant writhing pulsation of its surface.

After a while they would break the egg, and no one ever saw just how they did it. Almost always it took them half an hour or longer. On the rare occasions when they broke it in a few minutes, the sailors felt cheated.

When the egg was broken, the rats would eat it. Afterward they would not fly at a man's finger with anything like their former enthusiasm. For that reason the mamasan seldom gave them their egg until about an hour before closing time.

I did not spend as much time in bars as this particular reminiscence might seem to indicate. If for no better reason, I simply could not afford it. I found time to read many books, but seldom with the sense of consciously seeking enlightenment. I felt that I was reading for entertainment. Books were hard to come by, and I found entertainment in more than one unlikely volume. Some ships had no libraries. Others had only a few Western stories. I could not often afford to buy a new book. But in the thieves' market of Hong Kong I would sometimes find a few books for sale among the other junk. There was quite a good secondhand bookstore in Shanghai. And I soon learned that in the scores of cheap bookstores in Japanese cities there would usually be, far back in the rear, a few secondhand books in English.

Thus I did not lack for books, although I had to read a weirdly varied lot of them. Finding them in my trips ashore was one of my chief enjoyments. The only gripe I had was my trouble in keeping them once I had read them. Lockers for personal gear were designed to hold just the prescribed outfit of uniforms, provided they were rolled or folded very compactly. There was no room for books. I would hide books away in crannies all over the engineering spaces the way a squirrel hides acorns. When I trans-

ferred to a new ship, I would just have to leave most of them. Now that I live ashore I will not relinquish any book, and I have already had to move once to a larger house.

Very little of all that I read excited any sharply focused intellectual curiosity in me. An exception was the frequent references one encounters to Nietzsche's statement that God is dead. That seemed to me a pretty enormous thought. I knew a beachcomber in Guam, a towering old Englishman who was said to have once been a scholar at Oxford, and I asked him about it. He confirmed the statement, but he could not explain it. He gave me a worn copy of *Thus Spake Zarathustra*, to which I clung through three transfers, but I never did succeed in understanding it. I did not really try very hard to understand it. I was content to read it as I did poetry, simply to enjoy the excitement and wonder it could arouse.

The turning point came for me with World War II, when I was twenty-eight years old. I had long intended to serve out my twenty years and retire in the Orient, as many men did in those old days. When I had to return to the States, with the uneasy conviction that those old days were gone forever, it was not pleasant. My future was suddenly all uncertain. I had let myself become too deeply aware of the common humanity I shared with Chinese and Japanese to force myself easily into the mental and emotional state proper to wartime. My ship came into San Francisco in March of 1942 at the time when Americans of Japanese ancestry were being dispossessed and imprisoned. The mood of the people, as I sampled it in the places where I went ashore, seemed to me almost that of a lynch mob. A few unpleasant experiences quickly taught me that it was dangerous to speak my thoughts and possibly a sin even to think them. I had to relieve my feelings with drunken mutterings to which no one listened. I ached with self-contempt and a shattering sense of opposed loyalties which I could not reconcile. I was undergoing a genuine crisis of faith, and I began dimly to understand at last what Nietzsche was talking about.

I went all through the war in that state. Thinking back to it now, I am reminded of a verse from Kipling:

> It is not learning, grace nor gear,
>   Nor easy meat and drink,
> But bitter pinch of pain and fear
>   Which makes creation think.

For it was then for the first time in my life that I began to think, deliberately to think, as clearly and as coldly as I could. For the first time I began to read books in clear, conscious pursuit of the thought in them. I was no longer seeking entertainment only, but information and the hope of a way out of pain. I would no longer skip over a difficult passage after a brief puzzlement. I would worry at it for an hour and only leave it undigested, if I had to, with a sense of baffled defeat. I was gaining an entirely new conception of the nature of books and the way a man must read them.

The time was propitious for that change in my bent. The men around me were a cross section of civilian America temporarily in uniform, and there was always someone with whom I could discuss ideas. With my modest share of wartime prosperity, I could buy any book that I wanted. The paperbound Armed Services Editions began coming aboard ship. Few of them were froth and many were very solid books indeed. I had never before read so many books of worth and substance, one after another. And one of those Armed Services paperbacks, I thought privately at the time, almost literally saved my life. Now I think a more accurate word would be *salvaged*.

That book was Thoreau's *Walden*. I know it has long meant much to many people. But I doubt whether it has often happened that *Walden*, or any other book, has come so providentially into the hands of a man so desperately in need of it. It showed me a middle way between trying to be a Nietzschean herdman and trying to be a Nietzschean superman and failing at both. It not only gave me back my sense of personal worth and significance; it established that sense more firmly in me than I had ever had it

since I had become a man. For the first time since childhood I knew again certainly that I had a right to exist, that I really did exist. I could read *Walden* with the emotional response proper to poetry and at the same time understand it rationally. The book seemed to me so radically subversive that I wondered how it could be permitted aboard any ship in wartime.

Well, I will not go on about *Walden*. No doubt I have read many a better book when I was not so peculiarly ready to make a total response to it. Perhaps it is possible to have a book-experience such as mine with *Walden* only once in a lifetime, and a great many other books can trigger and serve it. But for me it was *Walden*, and from it I shaped a new future for myself. I planned to retire from the Navy to a cabin in the Nevada desert, stock it with books, and live there as simply and richly as Thoreau had lived by Walden Pond. I began accumulating books for that purpose. I went on reading books with an even stronger will to know and to understand.

And now at last I come to something I hope may be of genuine professional interest. My design was to gain a formal education, to acquaint myself with all areas of thought, simply by reading books. I kept at it year after year, I was very resolute about it, and in the end I had to acknowledge failure. I was forced to conclude that, for me at least, there was no substitute for a college education.

I met books that I could not read. I spent months on some of them. I suspected that the treasure they withheld from me was proportional in richness to the difficulty of getting at it. I would start over again and again, trying to pinpoint the precise page and then the paragraph and finally the single word at which my comprehension began to fail. I would squint and scratch my head and chew my pencil. I would writhe my feet and ankles in among the rungs of my chair, and sometimes I would grip a book hard enough to tear it. When the unconscious physical expression of my frustration reached that pitch, I would become conscious of it and relax and laugh.

At those times I would be irresistibly reminded of the Hong Kong rats so frantic to break their egg. Once I had laughed at them, and now by some transhuman justice I was in their predicament. No rats were present to laugh at me, so I laughed for them.

To begin with, I had thought a dictionary would be all the help I would need. I did not give up that notion easily. I don't know how many times I looked up the word *ontology* and grasped at it as futilely as the Hong Kong rats would bite at their egg. I used to go into bookstores and look up that word in every dictionary they had, vowing to buy the first one in which I could understand the definition. I never found such a dictionary.

What I did discover was the existence of a kind of vocabulary of higher order, a fundamental outfit of ideas which the writers of the books I could not read assumed that their readers possessed. The ideas would appear on the printed page only as a casual reference or a literary allusion, yet a full knowledge of them was necessary in order to follow the author's argument. I began to understand it as a kind of shorthand of thought which permitted the author to convey to the initiated clearly on one page what might require fifty pages to make clear to my more limited comprehension. It was not enough to be literate in letters; one had also to be literate in ideas. When I had learned that the hard way, I decided that I must attend a university before retiring to my desert Walden.

I knew that it would require several years, but I expected it to save me a great deal of time in the long run. I meant to come out of it equipped to read and understand in a week, books that might otherwise tantalize me for a month and evade me at the end of it. I meant to develop a metaphorical set of teeth and gape of jaw that could crack any egg in print.

Let me say that I found the University of North Carolina abundantly able to supply what I lacked. I can now read almost any book in English that I wish to read. In addition, I can tell quite soon whether any particular book is to me worth reading. I no longer assume that anything difficult is good for me in direct

proportion to its turgid impenetrability. I remember ruefully now certain almost worthless books into which I poured Herculean efforts in the old days. Those eggs were shell all the way to the center. Nothing like that can fool me now.

Thus I found the University of North Carolina able to supply what I knew I lacked. But I found here also other gains for which I had not bargained. I discovered other lacks of mine which I had not been cognizant of until I knew they were being supplied. And I now think those were the more important.

Each new thing I learned seemed to fit as a bridge between two things that I already knew. I had brought to the University a great, chaotic rat-hoard of miscellaneous information. As my studies progressed, I could appreciate how it was all being subtly rearranged into some kind of form and order. It was being made more useful and available to me and charged with renewed interest. It took me more than a year to understand clearly what was happening, and then I learned the principle of the organizing scheme. I put to myself the problem of how to state in one sentence what I hoped to gain from the University. The answer was no longer that I wanted to learn how to read books. The new answer was itself a question: What is a man? The answer to that question was what I sought both from the University and from all the books I meant to read afterward.

From the moment I began my studies, the appearance of the world began to alter for me. I mean that quite literally. I started the summer of 1953 with a course in physical geology. I was fascinated to learn the origin and history of land forms. The many slow processes that were shaping the face of the earth all around me, hitherto unknown and unnoticed, caught my eye everywhere I walked. There was a granite boulder in front of Battle Dorm that was a perfect example of spheroidal weathering. I passed it every morning and nodded to it. Sometimes, walking home up Franklin Street in a heavy rain, I would loiter for half an hour to watch part of the life history of a river valley in a rivulet cutting across the gravel sidewalk. In my mind I might be assisting

at the creation of the Grand Canyon of the Colorado. Thus the simplest, most unregarded things took on a new and vital interest for me. It pleased me to see change everywhere in seeming permanence. Nothing is fixed. Nothing lasts forever. That was what those poetic symbols of permanence, the very rocks themselves, were saying in stony dumb show. There is nothing like physical geology to stretch a man's time sense out to the breaking point.

Almost every course I took added its own kind of increment to the process I am describing. I have time here to mention only a few of them. For instance, that same beginning summer I took English 21 and discovered *Paradise Lost*. We were required to read only parts of it, but I read it all and some parts repeatedly. Later, in a full semester course on Milton, *Paradise Lost* became and remains for me one of the finest approaches to the secret of What is a man? that I am ever likely to find in English. But at first encounter, even with the aid of the University, I could not crack that shell.

With my first fall semester I continued geology and started botany. Botany opened for me new windows on living things. Insensibly through the years my vision had been dulled by familiarity. I looked through a microscope into the fine structure of leaves and flowers and stems. I discovered the whole world of meaningful form and color, of beauty and wonder, that lies beyond the reach of natural human vision. The cumulative experience of it sharpened my natural vision to a finer discrimination than it had ever had. What had before been a mass of unregarded green all around me as I walked became a crowding of individual forms all beautifully interrelated and full of meaning. With natural vision, we see only surfaces and infer solidity. In the strangest kind of way I felt that I was learning to see in three and even in four dimensions. In the same way that I could see solidity by inference, I began almost seeing down into the piled strata of the earth, into the busy microstructure of leaves and flowers, back through time to the seed of a plant or the form of a hill a million

years ago. That vision of the mind's eye fused unbidden with the natural vision and infused the whole with wonder. I thought how William Blake could see the world in a grain of sand and heaven in a wild flower, and I suspected that I might have broken into that realm of poetic experience through a door not open to men until the last few generations.

By the time I knew surely that I was seeking the answer to What is a man? I was almost through with the physical sciences and well launched into the social sciences. Anthropology was another great breakthrough for me, this time through the screen of stereotyped familiarity hiding from me man and his works. It taught me new ways to look at familiar experiences. That was true of all that I learned in the University. In some measure, great or small, each course contributed to making all things new. It even made the past new. All of my memories cried out for re-working under a different light, one I had not known how to cast on them before. As I had begun by pestering Dr. White with questions about land forms remembered from my travels, so I ended by pestering Dr. Honigmann with my reminiscences of military life in China. For one term paper we were asked to write a brief anthropological description of our home towns. I had been so long gone from my home town that I wrote up a ship instead. I am now expanding that term paper into my second novel.

I never did expect to learn any final or complete answer to What is a man? I would almost instinctively have rejected any that was offered me. The nearest thing I have to an absolute conviction is the sense that man himself is neither final nor complete and never will be in all of linear time. I always knew that I would have to put together the most satisfactory master-answer that I could from my own insights and the partial answers I could learn from other men and their books. I sought as many partial answers as I could get from science, because science is not shackled to absolutes. When some seemingly fundamental principle of science requires revision, the scientists are free to revise it or

scrap it without the necessity of burning large numbers of help-less people. Science leaves man room to grow and to go on dis-covering himself.

I was graduated from the University seven years ago and I am still busy on my quest and I do not expect to complete it any time soon. One of the many partial answers I learned in the Uni-versity, however, has become so important a foundation stone for me that I would like to give it specific mention here. I found it in Dr. McCurdy's course on Personality. It is the concept of a man named Andras Angyal, who deserves to be better known than he is. He requires the whole of a rather difficult book to develop it fully, so of course I cannot hope to present it ade-quately in a paragraph, but I will try.

Briefly and baldly, then, any human life from birth to death can be understood as a gestalt in time. The linear sequence of any man's experience and behavior forms a meaningful pattern, just as do the sequential notes of a musical composition. They form a mosaic distributed in time rather than in space. The ar-rangement is governed by the same principles as a spatial gestalt, and closure can come only with death. A human life is an inte-grated whole which is more than the sum of its parts. But the wholeness is not achieved, nor is the final degree of integration achieved, until death. Therefore any experience, no matter how far back it seems to lie along the time-track, is not complete either. It will not be complete until the gestalt is closed and each experience making it up is given its final significance by virtue of its place in and contribution to the whole.

The individual human past is not immutable. Everything in it is still happening and will not cease to happen until the gestalt is closed. Every past experience is subject to change, as the con-figuration of the forming whole is changed. Each man of us is living his own personal work of art, cannot avoid doing so, can-not evade artistic responsibility for his product, because that is one of the fundamental consequences of being human.

When I first met that thought I found it a very huge one. I

have since improved my grip upon it by alternate approaches through existential philosophy, but it is still the scientific formulation of it which for me affords the most conviction. It is not a new thought. I realize now that I met a form of it, once in the days before I came here, in Bergson's *Creative Evolution*. That book was one of the eggs I could not crack. The thought is older than Bergson. It is contained in the proverb "While there's life there's hope," which no doubt goes back almost to the dawn of language. I never fully understood that proverb, simple as it is. It was just words. I know also that there are older and more traditional paths to something which at bottom is probably much the same as Angyal's concept, but I never found much conviction along those paths. All through this talk I have been describing the paths that I did find open. If I had come away from the University of North Carolina with nothing more than that one key bit of wisdom, my time and money would still have been very well spent.

Such wisdom as I have gained tells me that it would be wise if I stopped at this point. But I feel obliged to comment, however briefly, on the current [1962] controversy over American education. I will not be as bold as Admiral Rickover. I have already said as much as I know of my own knowledge: that there is no easy and perhaps no possible substitute for a university education to forward a man along the way I wanted to go in the world. I have affirmed that for me the University of North Carolina was all that I had expected and far more. But I could not help knowing that many of the youngsters in the classes I attended were not finding it anything like the enthralling experience it was to me. I observed only those few who chanced to sit near me in class and to whom I sometimes talked. I have not thought at all deeply about what I observed, and what I have to convey is no more than an impression.

Overwhelmingly, my impression was of passiveness. Some of the boys seemed dutifully to sit there expecting the professors to

give them an education much as they would expect a barber to give them a haircut. Others sat braced as grimly as they might in a dentist's chair. They were finding it unpleasant, but they were going to sweat it out. Whatever the emotional tone, however, the attitude seemed predominantly passive. They were undergoing an education, not undertaking it.

What I am calling passiveness is more a subtle and deeply-founded quality than I can readily convey. Probably no adjuration from without nor anything less than the most desperate act of will from within can much relieve or change it. It seems to be a kind of fundamental life-attitude which colors all effort, no matter how great. I sometimes think it springs from a self-identity founded on thingness, on a sense of the self as object, plastic to events which happen to it. There is possible another sense of the self as process, as continuous event, over which the man has a measure of control and for which he has a full measure of responsibility. Probably they are complementary aspects of something unstatable in words, and too much one-sidedness either way might be regrettable. I just do not know enough to talk about it.

Even the best and most eager of the students I observed, however, seemed not to be free of what I am calling passiveness. In some measure they were all doing what was expected of them, and as a reward for it they expected to receive their education gift-wrapped in a piece of parchment at graduation. They seemed to lack the full pleasure of discovering their education as they went, of living it day by day, of being lured on by the continuous exhilarating wonder of it, knowing no greater lure than that.

In my own thinking I link that passiveness with underdeveloped imagination. I am more pessimistic than Admiral Rickover. I fear it will not be enough, no matter how expertly Johnny learns to read, unless he also learns to read creatively. By reading creatively, or by listening creatively to a lecture, I mean getting up the same order of spiritual sweat as the writer or lecturer. I mean trying desperately to match him stride for stride instead

of assuming that it is possible to get there by riding on his back. Those who can do it already will know what I mean; no amount of verbal amplification can make it clear to those trapped too much in passiveness.

I fear also that, increasingly these days, Johnny takes his bent toward passiveness and away from imagination long before he encounters the alphabet. His toys grow more elaborate and differentiated each year, restricting the freedom of his imagination. They tend to pre-program his play. His dolls and teddy bears and monsters are becoming animated and vocal with batteries and transistors. They no longer give him even the small pleasure and reassurance of winding up a spring. The toys are threatening to become more real than the children.

Yet if he did not have such toys, any normal child could make do with a stick and a tin pot and a bundle of rags transfigured to order for any play-occasion by the unhampered power of his developing imagination. In healthy measure his toys would be his own creations. His play-worlds would be his own creations with himself in command of them instead of subject to them. Soon enough anyway the adult thing-world would close in on him. But if he had been able to play creatively, he might find it easier later in life to read and to listen and to look at the world creatively.

What I have just said springs from too insufficient a base of observation to be taken at all seriously. It is the most tentative of suggestions. I have already talked myself into a position where I may be accused of wanting to shoot Santa Claus and bring American children up like starving rats. So I had better pipe down and batten my hatches.

From a speech before the North Carolina Library Association, Durham, N. C., October 25, 1963

Adventures with Libraries

～ LIBRARIES have always been very important to me, and I am pleased to have a chance to express my gratitude for libraries as an institution and to librarians as a vitally helpful and important category of people in the world. I mean these remarks to be more entertaining than instructive, although I may pause here and there to point a moral or adorn a tale. But mainly I will just talk in a rambling way about some adventures I have had with books, libraries, and librarians.

I might say to begin with, in order to assure you that I am not just being conventionally polite, that I married a librarian, and I chose to make my home in Chapel Hill in large part because of the presence there of the Wilson Library. That has been my greatest and most joyful adventure to date, and it is still going on. But, to paraphrase Kipling's soldier, I have had to take my books where I found them, and I had met many libraries before I came to Chapel Hill.

Some of them were rather strange libraries. In a Buddhist temple in Japan I once saw a library containing the six thousand or so sacred books of Buddhism. Each book was a small packet something like a folding set of souvenir postcards, so that is not really as much reading as it sounds as if it were. The structure that held them was an eight-sided contraption somewhat higher than my head. It was balanced and mounted on a pivot, and for a small fee you could take hold of a bar and push it around in a circle on its axis. When you had taken it around three times, you earned the merit of having read all the books.

Standing there with a shipmate, I watched it sway and creak as Japanese trudged dutifully round and round with it like Samson, eyeless in Gaza, at the mill with slaves, and we wondered about the philosophy of it. It did not seem to matter which way they went round with it, and we supposed some of them might be earning extra merit by reading all the books backward. Finally, I paid a double fee and took it around six times so as to have the merit of having read all the books twice. Afterward I did not feel any different, except that I was breathing heavily from the exertion. My shipmate told me that I was out of condition and that I should have known better than to try to read so rapidly.

There were libraries of another strange sort to be found in China in those days. I think I saw a number of them before I knew what they were. The first one I recognized was a niche in the street side of a stone wall bounding a temple courtyard in Amoy. It was stuffed with newspapers, and I saw a skinny, ragged coolie come up and put in some more torn and folded papers. Right behind him came a fat little man in a gown, who picked through the collection and carried several things away. In those days I was always alert for something to read, so I went over to see what was there. It was mostly flimsy gray Chinese newspapers and magazines, but there were also old handbills and posters and Golden Bat cigarette boxes. The only thing in English, apart from an empty and crumpled Camel cigarette package, was an old copy of the *South China Morning Post*, a Hong Kong newspaper. I glanced through it and then put it back to await the next customer.

Later I learned that such public repositories for printed matter were quite common in the older, more backward sections of Chinese cities. Generally they were large baskets woven of palm fiber or rattan. They sat in certain sheltered corners, and you would take them to be litter baskets looking peculiarly futile in such foul and messy streets. But they were not there to protect the streets from scrap paper; they were there to protect scrap

paper from the filth of the streets. Chinese ideographs painted on them appealed to passers-by to "Respectfully Have Pity on Printed Paper."

Anyone who rescued printed matter from the street and put it into the basket gained merit thereby. So did anyone who took it out of the basket and carried it home to read. People who had printed matter to dispose of were expected to put it into those baskets rather than to throw it into the street with the other household rubbish. At regular intervals certain pious persons would carry away what no one wanted and decently burn it, as we dispose of worn-out American flags in this country.

It has been said often enough that the heathen Chinee is peculiar, and certainly one of his outstanding peculiarities is reverence for the printed word. During the nineteenth century there were numerous destructive riots because foreign devils misused printed paper. At least one missionary lost his life because he had put printed paper to what the Chinese considered a degrading use. A century of battering had made China much more civilized by the time I reached there, but a lingering reverence for the written word was still in evidence. For instance, the Chinese aboard the Yangtze River gunboat on which I spent several years would go out of their way to show me unusual marks of respect, although many other Americans aboard that ship were more powerful than I and in a better position to do them favors. It was the fact that I was always reading books which made extra "face" for me with the Chinese.

I will not here go deeply into my thoughts on that topic. Let me note only that the reverence extended to *all* written words, whatever the language, and that it was felt perhaps most strongly by people who were themselves illiterate. And I wonder whether the Americans of a hundred years ago, when very many of us were illiterate, may not have had a greater respect for books than we find among ourselves nowadays. I am sure that all of you can tell horror stories about mistreated books. One of the most disturbing that I have heard concerns a student at the University

of North Carolina, a personable, engaging, well-connected young man, who was found to be tearing pages out of bound volumes of magazines. He excused himself by saying that, since they were only magazines, he thought it did not matter. I try to believe his statement to be a feeble lie, the best that he could think up on the spur of the moment. But sometimes I fear that that young heir to all the ages may have been telling the simple truth: he really did not know it mattered, and then I shudder all over. And I reflect that it might not be amiss if we were to copy a certain barbarism from the Chinese and to post in our libraries signs appealing to such as he: "Respectfully Have Pity on Printed Paper."

Let me turn now to the sort of libraries with which we are all more familiar. It was my good fortune that the isolated little desert town in which I grew up had a good public library. That was due to the foresight and energy of several women's clubs, whose members obtained a Carnegie grant and built the library in 1908, while most other small towns of that newly and sparsely settled region still did not have public libraries a generation later. It was a rectangular brick building with wide eaves and a neat little porticoed entrance, and it sat upon a terraced lawn. I can remember seeing it as a preschool child, and I may even have heard it called a library, but the word "library" meant nothing to me then. I did not know that it had books inside.

When I learned to read in school, I quickly developed a thirst for reading. Whether I understood it or not, I read everything I could get hold of. I could not get hold of much. I lived on a small farm isolated in the sagebrush, and we had only a few books at home. We took the local weekly newspaper and a farm magazine. On my way home from school I would pick up any old newspaper or magazine that I saw blowing around and carry it home to read. That went on for several years, until I was in the fourth grade, and I cannot now understand why I did not learn sooner about the library.

I do not remember now who did finally tell me about the library, but I remember very vividly my first visit there, one day after school in early spring. I was a shy, silent boy, very much afraid of people, and I walked past the library several times before I found the courage to go up the steps and through the heavy glass doors. I had my opening sentence all composed, rehearsed, and ready in my mind, but I was thrown off poise to find that I had only reached a kind of entrance hall, the landing of a staircase. I had to go up some more steps and through a pair of lighter glass doors before I would be really inside. I hesitated for some moments, but through the second set of doors I could already see more books than I had ever dreamed existed, so I got my sentence ready again and went on in.

No one was inside except the librarian, behind the check-out desk to the right. She was a plump, pleasant-looking woman, and she smiled at me. I stammered out my sentence, something about could I please have a book to take home and read. She asked my name and age and made out a borrower's card for me, and then she explained that I would have to get two property owners to sign it before it would be any good. She made two little x-marks where they were to sign.

I did not understand. I had never heard the term "property owner." I did not think I knew any property owners. I began to suspect that the rules of that library were rigged in a way to shut me out of it after all. Something of what I was feeling must have shown in my face, because the librarian smiled and told me very gently that she would take care of having the card signed for me. She said I could take a book away with me right then, if I wanted to.

I felt a surge of gratitude and of love for her, and I had to struggle to keep from crying. Her name was Mrs. Sessions. She has long since passed away, but as long as I live I will remember her as fondly as any person I have ever known.

Thousands of books lined three sides of the large room. It did not seem possible to choose one. I stood before them, and my eyes

raced across the titles, reading one here, one there, as I tried at
the same time to look at them all at once and at each one individually. Finally one title on an upper shelf stopped my eye. It
was Blasco Ibáñez' *Four Horsemen of the Apocalypse.*

It happened that the movie made from that novel, starring
Rudolph Valentino, was then playing in the one theater of our
town. The advertising posters for it showed four spectral horsemen riding through the sky above flaming cities and a stricken
land. I thought it was about actual ghostly riders in the sky,
which appealed strongly to a romantic strain in my imagination,
and I would have liked very much to see that movie. But I never
had the price of a movie in those days—I was lucky to see one once
a year—and I had long been resigned to foregoing movies.

While I gazed at the Ibáñez novel, a kind of illumination came
to me. I suppose I had known vaguely before that there was a
connection between books and movies, that a book could be
another form of a movie, but I had never thought about it. Suddenly it seemed to me that a library was like a town with thousands of movies all showing at once, and you could go to any one
you wished at any time or place that pleased you, and the others
would all still be showing any time you wanted to see them, and,
best of all, it did not cost anything. I felt suddenly free and
wealthy, as if I had found my way into a cave full of treasure. I
think from that moment I stopped feeling sorry for myself because I could not afford to go to movies.

That was my first impression of a library, as a nine-year-old
boy. I suspect it may still linger somewhere beneath all my later
impressions, because I go to scarcely more movies nowadays than
I did then, and I read as many books as ever.

The Ibáñez novel was too high for my reach, and I asked Mrs.
Sessions to take it down for me. When she learned why I wanted
it, she told me that it had nothing to do with ghost riders in the
sky and that I would probably find something more interesting
among the children's books. She led me to the alcove where they

were kept. I went willingly. I wanted to do anything she wanted me to do, because she was the lady who had charge of all the books. The book I finally carried home with me was *Rebecca of Sunnybrook Farm*.

My initial visit to that library was one of the crucial encounters of my life. Until I finished high school I was constantly in the library. I read all of the fiction and very nearly all of the non-fiction it contained. I believe that library contributed to my early education at least as much as did the public school. So, speaking from my own experience, I know that a public library can make possible a kind of self-sustaining educational process which would require a whole battery of teachers, truant officers, and administrators to push through in schoolrooms. I would like to dwell on that thought for a moment.

The key factor in my experience, I believe now, was that I never felt that I was reading for self-improvement or for some kind of future reward or even to please anyone other than myself. I read only for immediate pleasure, as thoughtlessly and greedily as a four-year-old child munches cookies.

Sometimes Mrs. Sessions would tell me, "I think you might like this book." It turned out that I always did. She never said anything to the effect that a certain book would be good for me with the implication that, like medicine, it might be a bit unpleasant to take. She never made me feel that it would please *her*, if I read a certain book. So I read Edgar Rice Burroughs and James Oliver Curwood side by side with Charles Dickens and Herman Melville, without any awareness that the adult world made between them a distinction of literary worth. It may have been, although I do not remember it now, that Mrs. Sessions adroitly led me to the good books. But I do remember that when she got in a new Tarzan book she would save it under the desk for me and let me have it first. Only in high school did I begin to learn about distinctions of worth between books. By then I had

already read so many of the good books with innocent and unreflecting pleasure that I was not to be put off from them just because I was suddenly told that they were good for me and that therefore I had to read them.

I believe that any book, however trashy and ephemeral, is good for a child if he finds pleasure in reading it. Any book that helps him to form a habit of reading, that helps to make reading one of his deep and continuing needs, is good for him. Discrimination will come naturally in time, perhaps in the college years. An attempt to instill it too early in life may well put a youngster off books altogether and rob him of one of the chief advantages of being human.

At the start of my sophomore year in high school our English teacher asked all of us who had read a book that summer to hold up our hands. I held up my hand and in response to her question named as one of the books I had read *The Bridge of San Luis Rey*. It happened to be one of the intellectual sensations of the season, but Mrs. Sessions had not told me anything about that, and I was puzzled at my teacher's markedly pleased reaction. To me it was just another novel and not a very exciting one. There was a new teacher on the faculty that year, a young man. A few days later he spoke to me cordially, saying that he had heard about my reading *The Bridge of San Luis Rey*. He invited me to his apartment for a talk and to meet his wife. He said he had a lot of recent books which he would be glad to lend me.

Reluctantly and ill at ease, I went with him. His wife was very pretty. She served cookies and milk, and there were books all around the room. They both wanted to talk to me about *The Bridge of San Luis Rey*, and I could not understand what they were saying, much less put in any meaningful word of my own. It was all about philosophy and fate and the tragic sense of life. When he saw my mute embarrassment, the man began trying to explain about the tragic sense of life. That made it worse. Finally I mumbled some excuse and fled.

I left feeling that they believed I had not read the book at all

but was only claiming to have read it in order to attract favorable attention to myself. It was another moment of illumination for me, but not a pleasant one. I hated having to know that you could do a thing like that with books. I wondered whether what I had been doing with books was really to read them after all, since I did not know anything about the tragic sense of life. That teacher was a good, well-meaning young man, but thereafter I disliked him and avoided him as much as I could. And to this day I have not read anything else written by Thornton Wilder.

That brings me to my second point, about degrees and levels of comprehension. Many of the books I read as a child were far over my head. I do not remember that I was ever distressed or bored by my incomprehension. I would simply use my imagination to cobble some sort of coherent whole out of what I read, aware that I probably had some of it wrong, but enjoying my own imagination as much as that of the author. I did not feel that I had to understand everything completely. Such books gave me a lively sense of how much there was to discover and know in the world, a sense that I could go on reading forever and never come to any end of things.

Therefore I wonder about the wisdom of expecting and demanding too much comprehension from young people, perhaps even at the general college level. I am disturbed particularly by the trend toward abridging and simplifying the great books to the end that children may read the mangled remains with full comprehension. I think it is false merchandising to offer such condensed and predigested books under the titles of the genuine books which they purport to be. Undeniably, it does make it easier for children and adults alike to gain the merit of seeming to have read them. But I wonder how much longer it will be before we put all the great books into a revolving bookcase and just have the children push it three times around. Since we are the world's most technologically advanced society, we will no doubt install electric motors in our revolving bookcases, and our children will only have to push a button.

When I turned eighteen, I enlisted in the United States Navy. By then I was hopelessly addicted to reading. At each new place I went I would look up the library. I did not have any trouble finding books until I went to Goat Island in San Francisco Bay to await transfer to my first ship, which was stationed in the Far East. They had a very small library at Goat Island, but the rules were that no books could be checked out to transient personnel. I had about two months to wait there, so that was serious.

After a few days I found a store on Mission Street over in San Francisco which dealt exclusively in secondhand magazines. The old man who ran it would pay a penny each for magazines, and he sold them two for a nickel. It was a long, dusty, splintery old room with tens of thousands of magazines in crazy heaps on the floor. It was on the edge of the Skid Row district, and that was during the Great Depression and there were a lot of good men on Skid Row. They were always coming in with magazines to sell. They picked them out of garbage cans or from among the rubble on vacant lots or begged them from housewives. Plenty of other ragged men were always searching through the heaps for something to buy. That store did a thriving business.

I would spend an hour or so picking out a selection of ten magazines, pay a quarter for them, and carry them off to Goat Island. When I had read them I would bring them back, turn them in for a dime, and choose a new lot to take away with me. The thought came to me one day that the store really functioned as a library for the Skid Row men and some others like myself, a curious, low-grade, free enterprise sort of library, yet nonetheless a library. The old man who ran it remains one of my favorite librarians, although I never made any friendly contact with him or even so much as knew his name. He was an unshaven, taciturn, pipe-smoking old man, and between transactions he was always reading himself. He seemed to resent being disturbed in his reading by people who wanted to buy or sell.

I crossed the Pacific on the transport *Chaumont.* I had been told that all Navy ships had libraries, but I knew I would still be

transient on the *Chaumont* and unable to use its library. So I brought a dollar's worth of old magazines aboard with me and spread them evenly under the thin mattress of my bunk deep in a cargo hold. The men in the other bunks around me borrowed or stole the magazines, but sometimes they would put them back when they had read them. When I finally went aboard my own ship in Apra Harbor, Guam, I still had several unread.

That ship was going to be my home and community for at least two years, and I was most anxious for a look at its library. The library turned out to be a low bookcase, two shelves high, in a corner of the crew's compartment, where it made a handy place for the messcooks to set their coffeepots. It had glass doors that were locked, and inside there were only three books. One was entitled *Snow Man*, and I thought it might be a novel. The others were *Bowditch's Practical Navigator* and Volume Two of *The Collected Letters of Lafcadio Hearn*.

"Is that all the books you got on this ship?" I asked one of the older men.

"They used to be more. It used to be clear full," he said. "I don't know where they all went to."

"Guys left 'em laying around on deck and they got rained on," another man said.

Days went by, and I had nothing to read. I never saw the library unlocked. Someone told me I could get the key from the mail clerk. At first he denied having it, then remembered that his predecessor in the job might have given him such a key. He said he would look for it. Several days later he had not found it, and he made it clear by his manner that the key was lost for good.

I began developing an obsession about that book *Snow Man*. I wanted to read it. Every time I passed that way I would stop and look at it through the glass. Then, late one night, some men came back off liberty drunk and arguing. They woke everyone up with their shouting and shoving each other crashing against lockers. They were in that corner by the bookcase, and as I listened a

hope grew in me that I would hear the tinkle of breaking glass. But I did not hear it, and the confused melee moved away from there and began to subside. So I slipped on my shoes and went quietly over and kicked in the glass myself. In the morning everyone assumed that the drunks had done it.

Snow Man turned out not to be a novel, but it was quite an interesting book, and I read it several times.

I stayed on that ship four years, and later I served in other ships on the China Station, none of which had libraries that were much better. The best library I encountered in the Far East was in Cavite Navy Yard. They had quite a few books in a cool, quiet old stone building that had been erected by the Spanish hundreds of years before. I hardly ever saw anyone in there. A lot of the little house lizards called "geckoes" lived in the building. They made nests among the books, and they would run around on the ceiling eating flies and mosquitoes and making musical chirps.

Most of what I read were secondhand books that I bought ashore. In the early years my pay was very scanty and I had only a few dollars a month to spend on amusement, in which category I then mistakenly placed books. There were good secondhand bookstores in Shanghai and scattered lots of old books here and there in the other Asiatic ports. It became one of my chief pleasures ashore to search out books and to look at a great many of them and to decide slowly which ones, with prices within my reach, would afford me the most enjoyment. I think I learned in those days how many women feel when they buy hats and shoes. I am always able to buy clothing in a few minutes, but I still love to linger in delicious indecision in a bookstore. I can spend hours at it. And to this day I feel it wasteful to spend money on fine bindings or first editions or anything else except the actual printed pages. Some of the finest books I have read had lost their covers altogether by the time I met them.

Toward the end of the 1930's, after the Japanese occupation

of that region, a pirate publishing industry grew up in Shanghai. It became my main source of books. Pan-American had just pioneered flying the Pacific, and the pirates would have single copies of the popular new books flown out from the States. They would have pirated editions of them on sale all over Shanghai a week or more before the authorized editions arrived by ship from San Francisco. They even pirated *Reader's Digest* every month. They reproduced the books by lithography, using cheap paper and flimsy cloth bindings. Chinese money was being slowly inflated, so the resultant prices in U.S. money were incredibly low. Large books such as Hemingway's *For Whom the Bell Tolls* or Gunther's *Inside Asia* sold fresh off the press for about thirty cents.

The pirates seem to have moved to Formosa with Chiang Kai-shek, and they are still at it. Recently I received from Taiwan a copy of the pirated edition of *Sand Pebbles*, and it roused in me some pleasant old memories. My publishers wanted me to complain to my congressman, but I could not bring myself to do so. I had happily bought and read so many pirated books myself in the old days that I did not feel I had any moral grounds for complaint.

In the summer of 1937 I came back to the States for a few months and had my first encounter with a really large library. I had recently met on Guam a very old man who had a fascinating life story. I understand now that my novelist's instinct had seized upon his story, but all I knew at the time was that I was most anxious to learn more about it and to check what the old man had told me with other sources. His name was Henry Millenchamp, and he was the first child born in a mixed British and American colony which had settled about 1830 on the previously unclaimed and uninhabited Bonin Islands, north of Guam. It must have been an island paradise to the first child ever born there. He must have felt coeval with the land itself. Sometimes the little colony flew the British and sometimes the American flag, but neither nation would claim it. Then in 1853 Admiral

Perry came through with an American squadron on his way to blast Japan open to American trade. Perry accepted the islands as U.S. territory, also bought from the boy's father a tract of land on which to build a Naval coaling station, and practically stripped the little colony of livestock in order to provision his ships.

However, Congress failed to validate Perry's acceptance of the islands, and in the end the islanders did not even get paid for the provisions they had supplied. Japan, forced out of her centuries of seclusion, in 1870 took the islands for herself. Most of the colonists stayed and became Japanese, but Millenchamp moved his family to Guam, then a Spanish island. When I knew him, he lived among numerous descendants on an isolated jungle place north of Agana. He believed he had a valid claim on the United States for payment for some of Perry's purchases, but he had never been able to collect. He had a whole box of musty correspondence, including letters to his father from Presidents Fillmore and Pierce and from Admiral Perry.

The story of that little lost colony intrigued me immensely. When I found myself in San Francisco, I decided to go to the public library and see what more I could learn about it. I also wanted just to look at the library. When I started up the steps of that impressive building, I thought I was on the verge of experiencing the most breathtaking array of books I might ever see in my life.

Once inside, I was much taken aback to see no books at all. At first I did not know that the long row of little cabinets was a card catalog of all the books. I watched the people using it, however, and quickly understood how the system worked. I pulled open a drawer in the B's and looked randomly through the cards and began to reflect that two or three of those drawers, only a part of a single letter of the alphabet, would account for all the books in my home-town library. I looked again at the whole array of drawers, and it was a kind of substitute for the thrill I had been expecting, but it was not as good as seeing the books themselves.

Under *Bonin Islands* I found several references. By far the best of them was to a substantial section of Admiral Perry's book about his cruise to force open Japan. I went to the desk and asked a librarian if I might consult those books. She said I could look at all of them except the Perry book, the one I wanted most. It was classed as a rare book, and the rules stipulated that only scholars might look at it. I am sure that neither she nor I considered for a moment that a sailor might also be a scholar. I did not feel at all hurt or resentful. I had been a military man for six years, and I knew how it was about regulations. But the idea of a rare book was new to me, and I asked about it.

"It's been out of print a long time," the librarian said. "If it were lost or damaged, we would have to advertise for another copy, and we might not find one. It would cost a lot to replace."

"You mean like ten or twenty dollars?" I asked.

"Probably hundreds of dollars," she assured me.

She brought me the other books. There was not much in them. I went away from there remembering very vividly a copy of Perry's book which I had seen on sale for several years in a second-hand bookstore in Shanghai. That was before I knew about the Bonin Islands colony. It was a handsome, leather-bound book, and I would have liked to read it, but the price was about eight dollars in U.S. money, and that seemed to me impossibly high. Now, all of a sudden, it seemed very cheap.

In October I was back in China, reporting for duty aboard a coastal gunboat then in Shanghai. The Sino-Japanese fighting at Shanghai was in full swing, with guns going day and night and the debris of war floating down the river and searchlights and star shells all over the sky at night. The ships were not granting shore leave, but on my new ship there were no bunks, and I got special liberty for a few hours to go ashore and buy a canvas cot.

Once ashore, I headed directly for that bookstore. It was on Yu Yuen Road, which was an extension of Bubbling Well Road into a kind of no-man's-land that was always in dispute between the International Settlement and the Chinese. Italian Marines

were guarding that sector, and no one was supposed to go in there who was not a genuine resident. I explained to an Italian sergeant that I wished to visit my grandmother, who ran a bookstore. He said he knew her and she was a magnificent old lady. He let me through.

The bookstore was in the front part of a large Chinese house with courtyards and moongates. It was closed. I knocked on the door and rattled the knob. The old lady peeped out and recognized me and let me in. It turned out that she had sold the Perry book about a month before. I told her how I had learned in San Francisco that it was worth hundreds of dollars. She agreed sadly that it probably was, but how was she to know about such things? I felt as sad about it as she did. She gave me a cup of tea and we talked awhile. She said that the fighting was very bad for her business and she wished it would stop.

When the United States got into the fighting, after Pearl Harbor, I had never before had it so good in terms of books. The Red Cross and the AWVS would bring many bundles of magazines and boxes of books down to every warship leaving port. The paperbound Armed Services Editions began to be published, hundreds of very good books, and boxes of them came aboard regularly. Many civilians who liked to read and discuss books came into the Navy for the duration. It was during that period of book-plenty, beginning in my late twenties, that I began to discriminate in what I read, and I have been refining my discrimination ever since.

In 1944 my ship went around to the Atlantic, and I discovered the secondhand bookstores of New York. They remain one of my chief delights in that city. After the war, in 1949, I went to shore duty at Great Lakes, near Chicago, and there at last I learned to make genuine scholarly use of a library. I had a writing job in Public Information, and I made it the occasion to do a great deal of research in the library.

The library was the whole top floor of the administration building, in which my office was also located. It was a great, long room with books on all sides and bookshelves coming out at right angles to make a dozen secluded little reading alcoves along one side. The books were all catalogued, with detailed subject references. It was always quiet and relatively empty. I never saw more than eight or ten patrons up there at any one time. I did much of my writing up there because the quiet of the place and the presence of books all around seemed to stimulate my flow of thought and words.

There were two librarians, civilian women professionally trained, and from them I first learned a bit of how much art and science is contained in the profession of librarian. I could hardly believe that they themselves had made and now maintained that marvelous card catalog, which always seemed to lead me infallibly to what I needed. The two librarians had some Waves to help them. They also had a problem of a kind with which I hope no one here ever has to cope.

At that time there were many excess officers in the Navy, and shore jobs had been minutely subdivided in order to make positions for all of them. One such spare-gear officer had been put in charge of the library. He was a burly, florid man, who had been commissioned from the ranks during the war. I think his library job baffled him, and he resented the way the hush of the place seemed to daunt him. At intervals through the day he would clomp through the library, solemnly fingering for dust. He insisted that the Waves keep the tables and empty chairs in exact alignment. When he saw a sailor at one of the reading tables on a week day, he always suspected him of hiding out from work somewhere, and he would challenge the sailor to prove his right to be there. He knew I had a right to be there, but I think he felt I was overdoing it. He was always wanting to make disciplinary trouble for people with overdue books, and the two lady librarians hardly knew how to behave toward him. I was in the library

one Saturday afternoon when the clash of authority between them finally came to a head.

There was an excellent combined radio and record player on which the librarians sometimes kept instrumental music playing very softly. It was music that went with books. On that afternoon the officer-in-charge decided to listen to a World Series baseball game. He tuned it in, blastingly loud, then lit a cigar and settled grandly back to enjoy the game. I felt a surge of annoyance. But I had my own problem with that officer.

He outranked me, of course. On the other hand, I was on the staff and wrote speeches for the Admiral. I had constant, unmediated access to the Admiral, and it gave me the kind of unofficial power which must always be acknowledged and is always deeply resented by the people who are not themselves on the staff. I felt guilty about it, and it tended to make me much less self-assertive than I might otherwise have been. Not able to read, I stared at my book in angry indecision.

Then I saw the librarian on duty leave the desk with a resolute look on her face. She walked quietly over and turned the radio off. The officer came to his feet.

"Hey there, now!" he said protestingly, around his cigar.

He turned it on again, louder than ever. *Ball one . . . strike two . . . three men on base*, it was bellowing. It was shocking to hear that quiet, elegant radio roaring forth such stuff. The librarian argued with him. I could not hear what she said, but I could see her clenched fists and the embattled set of her shoulders. I could hear the officer well enough, however. He was shouting that this was the Navy and he was by God officer-in-charge and what he said went in that place. He was assuring her that any honest sailor would rather listen to the World Series than partake of any other delight afforded by this world or the next one.

"Go ask 'em! See if I ain't right!" he challenged her.

I stood up and walked over there and turned the radio off again.

"Look here," I told him. "I'm working on an important speech, and I can't do a thing with that racket going on. For God's sake, if you have to listen to that stuff, why don't you go down to the bowling alley?"

He flushed and bit into his cigar and did not answer. Instead, he turned and walked out.

I got along very well with those two librarians. It was they who finally procured for me, after a delay of thirteen years, the book by Admiral Perry that I wanted to read. They borrowed it for me from some university library. I read Perry's account of the Bonin Islands colony with scarcely diminished interest. By then I knew that I was going to become a writer when I retired. In the interval, however, Robert Standish had already written my novel about the lost colony in the Bonins. I still think Standish would have written a better book if he could have spent a few days talking with old Henry Millenchamp on Guam.

My next library, and it will probably remain *the* library for me now for as long as I live, was the Wilson Library in Chapel Hill. First as a student and later as an aspiring writer, I came to know it well. I could hardly function without it. With it, I have become familiar at last with one of the very large, top-level libraries of the United States. I have also done research in the New York Public Library, and I would not now have any qualms about approaching the Library of Congress and the National Archives.

So, again to paraphrase Kipling's soldier, I have taken my libraries where I found them, and I have come a long and round-about way. Just two months ago I returned for the first time in thirty-three years to the little desert town out West where I grew up. Of course I revisited my first library. It is still the same building, but it looked neat and quaint and small to me, oddly scaled down from the august appearance it had had for me as a boy. The present librarian is the wife of my old high school science

teacher, and she is a very understanding woman. She arranged for me to spend an hour on Sunday morning entirely alone in the library.

That was a memorable hour. I just walked around slowly, and slowly my old complex of feeling associated with that room pushed through into present awareness. It was more than memory. I sensed the actual presence of Mrs. Sessions behind the worn old desk, and from the corner of my eye I glimpsed a shadowy boy hunched at a table over a copy of *St. Nicholas* magazine. Forty years thinned away to gossamer. Nowhere else in that town was I able to re-experience the past half so poignantly.

Yet in some sort everywhere in that town and among my old schoolmates the spell of the past was strongly upon me and the lure and charm of the desert strongly renewed. I wondered again how I had come to settle in North Carolina rather than in that desert and mountain country where the world had begun for me. I knew that some strong, sure instinct had guided me, and I had already rationalized it in various ways, but on that morning it seemed to me that I could also rationalize it in terms of libraries. And I think that what went through my head that morning will serve as a fitting conclusion to my remarks here today.

A library is fundamentally a collection of books. I sometimes call my personal library an extension of my mind, a concrete and visible aspect of my mind. When I first visit the home of a new acquaintance and have a moment free to do so, I will go and read the titles of his books. I do not feel that it is at all impertinent. I feel that I am then in genuine communication with him, learning to know him better, discovering what ground we have in common. If there are few or no books in his home, it means that we probably do not have much in common.

Similarly, I think that public and other institutionalized libraries are indexes to and visible aspects of the collective minds of the communities that maintain them. I would advise any man who wishes to take the cultural measure of a state, a county, or a town to judge it by its libraries. I do not think that libraries are

very often faked up as cultural status symbols. They are usually genuine organic parts of their communities, outgrowths from them. They require generations of slow growth. Only older communities, like older men, have had time to read and to value and to accumulate large numbers of books.

There was little room for books in the wagon trains that went out along the Oregon Trail. There are never many books, nor the time and inclination to read them, in a new and raw country. I was born in such a country, where the last Indian wars had been fought out in my father's generation. When I was a high school student, the first settler of our town still walked the streets with the scars of Indian arrow wounds upon his body. Communities are potentially immortal, and they mature slowly. But individual men age all too rapidly indeed.

Therefore, in my own maturity, I needed for my fulfillment an older, richer, more seasoned and mellow intellectual climate in which to undertake my work. I know I could have found it in many of the older states, but North Carolina is the state where I did actually happen to find it, and here I have found it abundantly. And for me, the best visible indications of that largely intangible quality which now binds me with hoops of steel to North Carolina are always going to be its bookstores and its libraries.

From a speech before the North Carolina English Teachers' Association, Chapel Hill, N. C., July 9, 1964

The Wreck of Uncle Josephus

❧ MY generation was graduated from high school into the teeth of the Great Depression. Sometimes I think the train of increasingly fat years that began for us with our entry into World War II tends to mask within us the memory of how lean and hungry those Depression years were. I cannot now recall any great feeling of dismay at giving up the thought of higher education and a professional career. The problem was much more starkly elemental: How to escape the iron pinch of enforced idleness and poverty and the terrible sense of personal unworth they generated. Because I was a boy then, eighteen, with a boy's intensity of emotional experience, I can say honestly that I escaped out of American civilian life with greater pleasure and relief than accompanied my escape back into it twenty-two years later.

Several years after I went to sea, I was serving in a gunboat of the South China Patrol. She carried a small Marine detachment. Those Marines had the worst of everything on that ship, which was no paradise for any of us. In those days there was great mutual hostility between sailors and Marines. We called them *sea-going bellhops* and they called us *swab jockeys*, and we had more colorful names for each other which are not repeatable here. I have since learned that such hostility was deliberately fostered from above during most of the nineteenth century. About twenty years before I was born, the policy had been officially reversed. The several military generations since that time had been told, over and over and over, that they were really all brothers-in-arms

together. Yet when I was old enough to go to sea, the tradition of mutual hostility remained almost unshaken.

I began to notice a certain Marine sitting in quiet corners about the decks, studying a set of pamphlets, and writing. He was taking a course from the International Correspondence Schools in Scranton, Pennsylvania. It caught my interest. I had done a lot of work in shipboard refrigeration, surmising bits and pieces of the theory behind it, and I wanted very much to learn it all. I had once written to ICS and had found the description of its course in refrigeration most tempting. There were thirty-six study assignments, each in a separately bound booklet of about a hundred pages, filled with tables and drawings, the set by itself making a wonderful reference library on refrigeration. The cost, unfortunately, was one hundred and eighty dollars—hopelessly beyond my reach.

I defied the social barrier across our little world and struck up an acquaintance with that Marine. He turned out to be a simple, friendly man happy to talk about his ICS course, which was in English grammar and composition. He was having trouble. In those days before transoceanic air mail, it took about three months for an exchange of correspondence between Scranton, Pennsylvania, and Swatow, China. Thus he always had half a dozen lessons in the pipeline, and he lived in dread of their coming back rejected. When that happened, his officer would stop his liberty ashore until he had redone them. The officer also stopped his liberty if he did not complete a new lesson every two weeks. At the moment he was several lessons behind, and he had not had any liberty in about four months. I was indignant.

"This is your personal business," I said. "What right does your officer have to restrict you?"

"He has to. It's a Corps regulation," the Marine told me. "The Corps pays for it, so—" He shrugged.

I learned from him that a Marine could take any ICS course he pleased and the Corps would pay for it, but the Corps would

also force him to complete it on schedule as grimly as it would send him to hit the beach on Iwo Jima. Skipping details, let me say here only that I began helping him with the course, and we became quite good friends. When he regained his liberty, we went ashore together. He was very grateful, and sometimes we discussed wistfully the possibility of his signing up for a course in refrigeration, I to prepare the lessons and he to sign and send them in. But we both feared that a sudden transfer might separate us, whereupon he would be stuck with the course and would never get ashore again.

My crossing of the uniform barrier despite old custom did not go unremarked by my shipmates. I took a lot of rather sharp-edged joking about it, as did the Marine among his people. Finally the petty officer I worked for, a much older man who dated back to before World War I, undertook to chide me seriously. I refused to be abashed.

"If I'd known the Marine Corps would pay for ICS courses, I would've joined them instead of the Navy," I told him. He was not pleased. "How come the Navy won't pay for 'em, if you think it's such a great outfit?" I challenged him.

His answer put me for the first time upon the trail of the story I wish to sketch out here. "The Navy used to. We used to have all kinds of schooling, only they done away with it," he said defensively. "That ICS stuff the gyrenes got, it's just something they salvaged out of the wreck of Uncle Josephus."

Every man in the Navy at that time knew at least the name of Uncle Josephus, although many could not have named the Secretary of the Navy then in office. Uncle Josephus had undeniably left his mark. He had shivered the timbers of the United States Navy so thoroughly that twenty years later they were still twitching with remembered outrage. As I recall it now, the impression of Uncle Josephus then current among sailors was curiously ambivalent. He came through as a defier of admirals and a trampler upon traditions, but less dangerous than ridiculous. He was made

to seem a meddling do-gooder with no practical sense at all about war, ships, and the sea. Particulars were few. He had prohibited drinking aboard warships. He did not approve of obscene tattoos. He had tried to put a chaplain aboard every ship. He had put out of bounds the waterfront dives and brothels in all the best liberty ports. Perhaps the crowning story was how he had made two pairs of pajamas part of the regulation uniform outfit and decreed that all sailors must wear them when they went to their hammocks. That story alone seemed to dispose of Uncle Josephus as a man to be taken seriously.

Yet my petty officer's chance remark set me to wondering very seriously about Uncle Josephus. Somewhat later, in a dusty corner of the library at Cavite, I stumbled upon a little brochure printed for recruiting purposes in 1919. It described the machinist's mate school then operated by the Navy. It ran for sixteen months without a break in a taxing fifty-hour-a-week schedule, and it was more than the equivalent of two years of post-high-school civilian vocational training. The students learned all the basic and many of the advanced skills of all the manifold crafts of artificers in metal. The best men came out master machinists and went to sea as first-class petty officers. Within a year they could expect to make chief, and within a few more years to be commissioned as engineer officers. Even the lower half of the class went to sea as second-class machinist's mates.

I had just recently made second-class machinist's mate myself, and it had taken me nearly six years. I knew that chief was still many years ahead of me and that it was the end of the road except for a very few men who might become warrant officers. The Navy still had a machinist's mate school, a three-month course, but scarcely one engineer in a hundred had been through it. The few of them I knew all said it was lost motion. I had myself gone to sea without any preliminary training, and I had picked up what I knew in the old apprentice fashion. What a paltry smattering that really was, despite my eagerness over six years, I realized when I read that brochure. In fact, when I finally retired after

twenty years as a Navy engineer, I still had not learned half of what that school designed by Uncle Josephus could have taught me in sixteen months.

The experience kindled in me an enduring interest in Uncle Josephus. It gave me a sense of how the workings of fate had caused me personally to lose, and to lose heavily, in what my petty officer had referred to so casually as *the wreck of Uncle Josephus*.

Since then I have learned quite a bit more about Uncle Josephus. Before he was wrecked, he managed to rake, hull, and dismast the United States Navy as never before in the history of that august and barnacled institution. To tell about it most effectively, I must first sketch in the historical background against which it took place. In my mind the story of Uncle Josephus really begins in 1850, when Herman Melville published his book *Whitejacket*.

Traditionally then, a sailor's life was always harsh and brutal. Traditionally, the men who lived it were always drunken brutes. Traditionally, the quality of the men made inevitable the quality of the life they lived. Traditionally, any man who dared put that proposition the other way round was in for a very bad time.

Herman Melville so dared. In 1843, stranded in Hawaii, he had enlisted as an ordinary seaman on the U.S. Frigate *United States* in order to get home. His book *Whitejacket* was an account of his cruise in her around Cape Horn to Norfolk. In it he described graphically the brutal and degraded life of the sailors, with especial emphasis on the practice of flogging, then an almost daily occurrence aboard American warships. There was at the time a small group of Naval officers who found the practice of flogging, and the collective assumption about human nature which underlay it, morally offensive. They were mostly juniors, and they had not a Chinaman's chance of getting the practice abolished until Herman Melville's book appeared. Then their leader saw to it that a copy went to every member of Congress.

Congress took up the matter, and a great storm broke over the land.

The storm raged pro and con in the newspapers and among the people. Melville was praised as a humane reporter and damned as an ingrate biting the hand which had fed him. The leader of the rebel Naval officers, Captain Uriah P. Levy, was praised as a man of great moral courage and damned as a Jew with dark motives of his own for subverting the American Way of Life. We had no admirals in those days, being still wary of permitting the emergence of a powerful and entrenched officer corps which might threaten our democratic liberties. Captain Levy was the first man of his faith to reach top rank in the Navy, but many a Naval captain senior to him came before Congress to testify in favor of flogging.

There is something about life at sea which breeds a bone-deep conservatism in the men who follow it. Those grizzled captains spoke truly from out their hearts' conviction when they said that only with flogging could discipline be maintained aboard warships. They predicted mutinies and bloodshed with weapons more lethal than the cat every time a ship put to sea, if flogging were abolished. They insisted that, except for a few agitators and troublemakers, the sailors themselves approved of flogging. They brought equally grizzled petty officers before Congress so to testify, also from their hearts. The petty officers said that, without the correction of flogging, the loafers and slackers among the crews could not be made to do a fair share of the work but would instead be taking a free ride at the expense of the good men.

I think it rather probable that, if a vote had then been taken among Navy enlisted men, it would have favored retaining the cat. Nevertheless, Congress abolished it.

The ships went to sea, and there were no mutinies. The die-hard floggers, unconvinced, thanked God for the United States Marines. Traditionally, the Marines had always been the standing army of those little warship worlds. Traditionally, the officers

lived aft. Traditionally, the Marines were always berthed just forward of the officers, insulating them from the crew. The Marines had custody of the ship's small arms. They stood armed sentry duty day and night outside the captain's cabin and at other strategic points about the ship. Traditionally, mutual hatred between sailors and Marines had always been officially encouraged so that the Marines, in case of a mutiny, would for the sake of their own lives side with the officers. Marines also guarded the brig and had custody of prisoners. Under the new dispensation, a sailor punished with a brig sentence in lieu of flogging could always fall down a ladder while being escorted by Marines. There was quite a bit of falling down ladders.

Under the old dispensation, flogging had a kind of harsh but wholesome Old Testament quality. All hands assembled on deck to witness it, the sailors in silence with their caps off as if at divine services, the Marines drawn up smartly in ranks and under arms. The ship's doctor stood by with authority to stop the punishment if it seemed more than the man's constitution could bear. The victims received a measured number of lashes applied in a prescribed manner, and then it was over and their shipmates were free to comfort them in any way they could. The ritual made it seem somehow impersonal, like the visitation of a natural force. Often enough the officer who had initiated the flogging would afterward give the victim a stiff drink of brandy from his private stock.

When the beating moved into the darkness belowdecks, out of sight and hearing and therefore out of mind to morally sensitive officers and civilians, without any set mode or limit, the wholesomeness went out of it. It became far more spiritually degrading to all concerned, including all the nice people sheltered from knowing about it. The traditional hatred between sailors and Marines became bitter as death. Any Marine caught alone ashore by several sailors, men from a different ship, utter strangers to him, risked being beaten to death just because of the uniform he wore.

After the Civil War we had admirals, but they seem not to have been much bothered by it. They were clinging to sail and trying to hold steam at arm's length while the rest of the world's navies steamed everywhere. Our own navy slumped to thirteenth in world rank, just behind China and just ahead of Denmark. In the eighteen-eighties we got into an argument with Chile and had to back down because the Chileans had us greatly outmatched in sea power.

The Chilean episode brought public attention back to the Navy. A disturbing fact emerged. American citizens had for a long time simply been refusing to serve in it. About 80 per cent of so-called American bluejackets could not even speak English. The personnel turnover was about 60 per cent a year. In every port, despite Marine sentries and other precautions, from 10 to 20 per cent of a ship's company would desert. The captain would have to ship such new men as he could find among those water-front rats who had starved back into willingness to go to sea again. War was shaping up with Spain, and Lloyd's of London gave odds on a Spanish victory because all the world knew that American warships were manned by the scum of the seven seas, loutish drunks and brutes who had to be prodded to their battle stations with Marine bayonets.

By 1898, as the Spanish learned to their cost, that situation had been much improved. About 1890 another group of rebel Naval officers had started a reform movement, their aim being to man American warships with American citizen-volunteers. They got rid of sail and brought running water and electricity and me-chanical refrigeration aboard the ships. They expanded the basic ration greatly beyond the traditional hardtack and salt beef. They made a major effort to disband the Marine Corps altogether as a demonstration of trust in the loyalty of American sailors. They failed in that, but they did force a redefinition of the Ma-rine Corps' primary function. Thereafter it was to be landing when occasion demanded and taking some inconvenient Chinese or Latin-American situation well into hand.

The Navy folk-mind has made Theodore Roosevelt the patron saint of that little social revolution that produced the New Navy. His birthday is probably still celebrated unofficially and clandestinely as Navy Day. There is no doubt that he helped mightily to bring into being a powerful new set of ships, and he must have at least approved the shift from scum to American citizens in the men who manned them. But therewith he only created more trouble.

Now the trouble was ashore. The hallowed collective assumptions would not give way before reality. Sailors ashore on liberty were still required to remain in uniform. Putting on civilian clothing was still taken as evidence of an intention to desert. Among respectable civilians the uniform still branded its wearer as scum, someone not to be admitted to any reputable place of public accommodation. Anyone who has read Kipling's ballad "Tommy," written about that time, will have savored the human feel of it:

> I went into a theatre as sober as could be,
> They gave a drunk civilian room, but 'adn't none for me.
> They sent me to the gallery . . .

and so on. It was far worse in America, as American sailors were quick to note when they went ashore in British ports. In all American seaports there were very crude vice districts, and to them American sailors ashore were rather rigidly restricted. It was of no interest to tradition-bound civilian minds what sort of human being might be inside the uniform. So, very humanly, many of the American citizens inside the uniform became indeed persons of relative moral unworth and found it a tolerable sort of life. But some few men made a fight of it.

The fight came to a head in 1903 in Newport, Rhode Island. A chief petty officer brought suit in a local court to force a respectable restaurant to serve him a meal. He lost and appealed, and in time his case reached the state supreme court. By then, the funds he and his shipmates had collected were gone and they

were in debt. They made a public appeal for contributions. Theodore Roosevelt, then President of the United States, loudly endorsed their aim and sent them his personal check for one hundred dollars. His action drew notice from the press, and there was a brief flurry of deploring prejudice and quoting Kipling in editorials. But the Supreme Court of Rhode Island successfully defended the social integrity of Rhode Island and sent that chief petty officer back to his proper place in the Newport stews.

Theodore Roosevelt had spoken out loudly his moral indignation, but he had not produced even a small stick. Several states did pass laws making it a misdemeanor to refuse service in any place of public accommodation to any American citizen solely because he was wearing an Army or Navy uniform. People generally became uneasy about the blatant signs reading NO MEN IN UNIFORM ALLOWED, and most of them were taken down. Less offensively visible methods of discrimination were substituted. The solution was curiously reminiscent of the abolition of flogging fifty years earlier. And now at last the stage was set for the grand entrance of Uncle Josephus.

Actually, his entrance was quite unassuming. He went to Washington and sat down at a desk. The admirals brought him stacks of purely routine letters and orders to be signed without reading, as was customary. Uncle Josephus patiently read them through, asked questions, made changes in some, would not sign others at all. The ruling group of admirals greatly admired Prussian military philosophy, and they had ready a plan to reorganize the Naval administration after the model of the Imperial German General Staff. Uncle Josephus said he thought they would wait awhile on that. He often left his desk to visit ships and shore stations, and on such trips he would stray off the red carpet and talk to just anyone he saw, without regard to protocol.

The story of Uncle Josephus in Washington is too rich and full to be encompassed here. I must follow only one line of it and that sketchily—the line of education and human relations. On

that line an early incident, trivial in itself, illuminates Uncle Josephus and foreshadows what was to come. He went to Newport, Rhode Island, and talked to groups of recruits at the Naval training station there. He was surprised to learn from the records that more than half of the men enlisting had not completed grammar school and many were barely literate. On the train trip back to Washington the admiral who accompanied him broached, with some embarrassment, a delicate subject. It seemed that Uncle Josephus had twice addressed groups of recruits as *young gentlemen*. That would not do. That would not do at all. Uncle Josephus asked dryly what forms of address were thought proper. Well, the admiral said, *boys . . . lads . . . sailors*.

Uncle Josephus seems to have been a shrewd and kindly man with an ability to inspire trust. Sailors would talk freely to him rather than freezing up and stammering out what they knew they were supposed to say. Uncle Josephus listened to what they said and remembered it. Once he talked to a boy from Kansas who had joined the Navy to see the world and in two years had not gotten beyond Norfolk. That, and many other such talks, came to his mind when he set himself to solve one of the Navy's most serious problems.

The problem was recruiting. For many years the Navy had been unable to recruit up to authorized strength. More than half of the young men who did enlist would not re-enlist. Desertion was common. The recruiting poster of the period read: *Join the Navy and See the World*. That was the sales pitch, but the product was not selling. Uncle Josephus knew that, in point of fact, the Navy had not made a foreign cruise since Teddy Roosevelt had sent the Great White Fleet around the world in 1906. He had learned also how, on that memorable cruise, only a few carefully selected sailors had been allowed to go ashore in most of the ports visited, it being axiomatic that if all hands were given liberty they would get drunk and wreck the place and leave a bad impression of the United States. Many of the sailors had gone clear around the world without once being allowed ashore, and it had

given rise to a sardonic revision of the recruiting slogan: *Join the Navy and See the World—through a Porthole.* Uncle Josephus summoned the admiral who was his aide for personnel and said they would have to do something to stimulate recruiting.

"Yes, *Sir*, Mr. Secretary!" the admiral said briskly. "We'll print up and set out a few thousand more of our posters . . ."

No, they would not do that, Uncle Josephus told him. Instead they would send the fleet on a cruise to Europe and make true the posters already on display.

Never before, the old hands said unbelievingly, had there been such a preposterous cruise of warships. Uncle Josephus wrote detailed orders. The sailors were to attend lectures on European history and geography. The officers were to prepare and give the lectures. In Europe all hands were to have liberty. Those who pleased would be free to head for the waterfront vice districts, just as they would in Newport, Rhode Island. But just in case the collective assumption that sailors by nature had no interests beyond that might be false, tours also were to be organized. Those who preferred it might go in parties away from their ships for days, to see Rome and Paris and Venice, to have pointed out and explained to them all the places of artistic or historical interest.

The result was a triumph for Uncle Josephus and bitter confusion for his adversaries, who had been telling him earnestly that only they really understood sailors. Most of the sailors chose to go on the tours, paying all their own expenses, by the way. Disciplinary trouble on the cruise was negligible, less than the usual rate in Newport, Rhode Island. More important still, recruiting picked up all over America, and the re-enlistment rate shot up to 85 per cent. Most important of all, an idea began forming in the mind of Uncle Josephus, and all the admirals who opposed him would never be able to talk him out of it.

Not all of the admirals opposed him, of course. There has never been a time when certain Naval officers did not dare to

question the sanctity of certain traditions, often to the disadvan-
tage of their careers. Uncle Josephus soon gathered around him
a group of such officers who understood and shared his philosophy. But what I may call the power-group admirals in general
opposed him, some of them quite emotionally. They were sup-
ported by important civilian power groups, for reasons which I
have time only to hint at here. For instance, Uncle Josephus cut
the price of gunpowder in half by threatening to make it himself,
which did not cause him to be loved in Delaware. He objected to
the collusive bidding whereby the United States steel companies
charged the United States Navy for armor plate double what they
charged the Japanese navy. At Pearl Harbor, the hulk of the battleship *Arizona*, sunk December 7, 1941, has been made into a
memorial shrine. Much sentiment revolves around it, and it ill
becomes any man to hold that lightly. But when I saw the *Arizona* last, on my way out to the Korean War, I could not help
knowing also that Uncle Josephus saved the taxpayers half a million dollars on her armor alone and thereby set off another round
of screams that he was destroying the fundamental liberties of
the American people.

Uncle Josephus really did strike at certain liberties hallowed
by ancient usage. For another instance, he demanded of Newport, Rhode Island, that it close down its vice district. The town
fathers pleaded the ancient autonomy of the New England Town
Meeting and refused. Very lucrative rentals were involved, accru-
ing to unidentified persons of power. The vice district boomed
on, with uniformed Newport policemen controlling the traffic of
sailors in and out of the houses. Uncle Josephus took up the big
stick which Theodore Roosevelt had somehow been unable to
lay his hand upon. He put the district out of bounds to Navy
men and sent shore patrols to enforce his order.

That is a commonplace practice nowadays, but it was a quite
daring and radical interference with free enterprise at the time
Uncle Josephus pioneered it. The vice district starved out, and
the lucrative rentals fell to nothing. The only way left for the

local Navy payroll to enter the economy of Newport, Rhode Island, was through the respectable places of public accommodation. Very soon that began to happen without any noticeable destruction of the social order.

Whether he ever said so or not, Uncle Josephus seems to have felt that human beings tend to become whatever is massively expected of them. He set himself radically to reconstruct the social stereotype of the United States bluejacket, and the means he used was education. He coined a new recruiting slogan: *Join the Navy and Learn a Trade,* and he moved to make it true by setting up a series of service schools, such as the one I have already mentioned for machinist's mates. The opposition admirals objected that men so superbly well trained as artificers would never be content to stay in the Navy when they could earn more and rise higher in civilian life. Uncle Josephus probably did not consider that necessarily a loss to America, but he moved to answer the objection by opening channels for the best men to enter and rise within the commissioned ranks of the Navy itself.

That raised a real storm. Upon the troubled waters Uncle Josephus promptly poured a storm more stormy still. He coined a second new recruiting slogan: *Every Battleship a School,* and he moved to make it also true. His aim was to bring every sailor as nearly as possible to the level of a high school education. Time for classes was in part to be found by doing away with certain colorful but outmoded all hands evolutions such as scrub-and-wash-clothes. Against the usual opposition, he had steam laundries installed in all the ships. The classes could be taught by such qualified enlisted men as were available, but the bulk of the teaching would fall upon the junior officers.

Many of them resented it bitterly. One angry young officer told Uncle Josephus to his face that it was beneath his dignity to become a schoolteacher. No doubt with a Carolina twinkle in his eye, Uncle Josephus reminded the angry young officer that it had not been beneath the dignity of his commander-in-chief, President Woodrow Wilson. More senior officers opposed it on philo-

sophical grounds. The opposition leader, Admiral Fiske, who was already wrestling gigantically with Uncle Josephus on other points of totem and tabu, became predictably upset about it. He insisted that sailors who knew history and literature, grammar and arithmetic, would no longer be willing to undertake the frequent and vital, but also very hard and dirty, job of coaling ship.

It happened that at the moment Uncle Josephus was coping with that problem and also wrestling with the civilian coal barons over converting the warships to burn oil. Anyone who supposes that he thereby drew support from the civilian oil barons does not know Uncle Josephus. He was wrestling even more fiercely with them over another issue. Certain oil deposits had been discovered by government geologists on federal lands, and Uncle Josephus was trying to withhold them from private exploitation. He wanted them to be set aside as Naval oil reserves, to be tapped only in wartime emergencies.

Uncle Josephus won all his wrestling matches. Years later, mellowed by age and retirement from out the heat of battle, Admiral Fiske was able to speak almost kindly of Uncle Josephus. But even then he could not refrain from putting his finger upon the fundamental flaw in the philosophy of his one-time adversary. Uncle Josephus, Admiral Fiske said sadly, persisted in thinking of education as an end in itself and not as a means to winning sea battles.

It is not possible to defend Uncle Josephus on that charge. He was a trustee of the University of North Carolina, with a lifelong interest in education, and he did indeed think of education as an end in itself. Therefore it was inevitable that he would in time turn a shrewd eye upon the Naval Academy.

He began by sending to the Naval Academy each year twenty-five men chosen from the ranks by competitive examination. Later he raised it to one hundred men yearly. Finally he tried to require that young men going to the Naval Academy by Congres-

sional appointment first spend one year in the ranks. That last he could not quite bring off. It was one of his few defeats.

He studied the curriculum at Annapolis and found it, in his opinion, deficient in the humanities. The English courses in particular he graded at about the level of a middling good high school. The English professor was traditionally a Naval officer with no particular qualifications for the post except that he wanted it. Sometimes, perhaps, it was his wife who wanted it, because the post traditionally carried with it free of all charges a very fine house on campus, staffed and maintained at government expense. Uncle Josephus decided that a civilian English scholar of outstanding reputation should have that post and brought down upon himself the usual storm of accusations that he was ruining the Navy. He asked Dr. C. Alphonso Smith of the University of North Carolina English Department to accept the post, warning him that he might meet with a rather chilly initial reception. When Dr. and Mrs. Smith reached Annapolis, they were told that the fine house had just been assigned to a different post, one still filled by a Naval officer, and that they would have to find what lodgings they could out in the town. Whereupon Uncle Josephus, I am pleased to report, did for once in his official Naval life come to the defense of old custom and tradition. He made sundry telephone calls and had that fine house reassigned to the English professor.

The wrecking of Uncle Josephus began when President Harding came into office with a new cabinet and set out to restore our nation to "normalcy," as he called it. Certain admirals had been waiting in the wings for their chance to return the Navy to normalcy. I have read often enough the name of Uncle Josephus' successor, but I can never remember it for more than an hour or two. What I did learn and do remember with pleasure is that Uncle Josephus proved in the main to be unwreckable. Unlike the nation, the United States Navy did *not* return to normalcy.

In his eight years Uncle Josephus had put his personal stamp too indelibly upon it. He had brought too many officers and men over to his own way of thinking. He had proved to the most hostile and skeptical the worth of too many of his innovations for the backlash of normalcy to undo it all. The elaborate trade schools he had founded were much reduced in scope, but they were not abolished. Commissioning directly from the ranks was stopped, but the hundred men from the ranks each year continued going to the Naval Academy. The liberalization of the curriculum there remained in force, and Dr. Smith became a much-loved and respected figure. The vice districts opened again in all the seaports but, as I have heard more than one old salt say nostalgically, they were nothing like as vicious as they had been in the good old days. And let me note here with particular pleasure that one serious attempt to wreck Uncle Josephus, the plan to loot the Naval oil reserves in the Teapot Dome affair, resulted in the frustration and serious embarrassment of the wreckers.

Often enough before him other men had spoken pious words about it, but Uncle Josephus worked powerfully with actions to remove the stigma of personal unworth traditionally attaching to the enlisted Naval uniform. After Uncle Josephus, it was never successfully reattached. Judges were never again permitted to sentence young delinquents to the Navy in lieu of prison or reform school. It remained official policy to enlist only American citizens of attested good character and to give more weight to good minds and levels of education than to strong backs and subservient graces of manner. That I consider to be Uncle Josephus' greatest achievement.

My Naval service began in 1931, ten years after Uncle Josephus. I never wore civilian clothes, and I never felt barred from any place of public accommodation in which I could afford to pay for what I wanted. That was initially in California. California was one of the states which for decades had had a public accommodations law. It was still being resisted, and the resistance was still being challenged. The hold-out places called themselves

clubs, and admission was to members only. Sailors and Marines would go there in civilian clothes and get membership cards and then come back in uniform in order to be thrown out. The lawyers who connived with them would then bring suit for personal and punitive damages, and there were tales of men on this ship and that who had been awarded various sums. To me and to most sailors of the time it seemed less a moral crusade than a rather shabby racket.

There were only a few such places, mostly of the nightclub type. Any man who wanted to enter them could do so by putting on civilian clothes which, post-Josephus, was no longer forbidden as being the first step toward desertion. In fact I thought it eminently sensible to require civilian dress in such places. That made it difficult for sailors and Marines to know whose social presence they were supposed to resent and so whom they were supposed to pick a fight with.

One very significant development stemming directly from Uncle Josephus must also be credited in part to the young women of America. During the thirties they began increasingly to disregard the collective assumption that no nice girl was ever seen with a sailor, and there were many marriages. Official policy still sharply discouraged marriage, in various ways and for various reasons which I have not time to go into here. Those pioneering married couples had a very rough time of it, but the trend continued and, I think in 1940, a small dependency allowance over and above military pay was granted to married men. That marked a final capitulation and began what I think of as the salvaging or vindication of Uncle Josephus.

During World War II and in the years following, the dependency allowance has been steadily increased, and all manner of fringe benefits have been added. More than half of the career men now are married, and they may choose to live anywhere they please as an integral part of the civilian community. They buy houses and furnish them in middle-class style and look forward

confidently to sending their children to college. Those of them with sufficient talent and ambition can look forward to a commission and the equivalent of a college education for themselves. Service schools have grown in number and scope beyond the fondest dreams of Uncle Josephus. A rich web of cross-ties has grown up between the Navy and the civilian educational system. I have long since lost count of them, as I have also lost count of the manifold other changes making for greater individual human worth and dignity within the uniform I wore so long myself. What I have not lost hold of is the conviction that what has come to pass is the flowering of a seed implanted first and ineradicably by Uncle Josephus.

In summary, I will try to restate my conviction as briefly and clearly as I can. I see it as one tiny strand in a process of historical change. I pick it up one hundred years ago with Herman Melville reporting upon his little warship-world, the U.S. Frigate *United States*. In that period, only the most desperate circumstances could force an American citizen to put on the uniform of a United States sailor. The moment he did so he became scum, if he was not in that category already. The collective assumption of his society worked upon him from without in whatever direction he might turn. It worked upon him even more terribly from within himself. The more genuinely loyal he was to the society which held that collective assumption about him, the more damnably it worked inside all his defenses to make him despise himself and to become scum in actuality. In order to man the warships sufficiently to go to sea, it was a common recourse to enlist Negro slaves, crediting their pay to their owners. And, as Melville tells us, such Negro slaves in a ship's company were often envied by their shipmates. Because they were valuable private property, they were commonly spared the extremities of insult, hazard, and hardship meted out to the men who presumably owned themselves.

The various reform movements subsequent to Melville and

Captain Levy accomplished much in an outward, material sense. None of them went to the heart of the matter. Possibly the reformers, and I include Theodore Roosevelt, simply could not understand. Possibly they understood well enough but considered it something immutably ordained at the time the limits of the seas were established. I will not presume to say. But I think that Uncle Josephus was the first man in our history really to go to the heart of it with more than pious words.

I believe that during Uncle Josephus' tenure of office, and as a result of certain beliefs about our common human nature which he both held and knew how to act upon, something very significant happened. A balance tipped, irreversibly. Some kind of metaphysical center of gravity crossed an invisible dividing line, and all the king's horsemen of normalcy could not thereafter nor ever will be able to shift it back again. Uncle Josephus, in short, was always really unwreckable.

I do not have sufficiently refined scholarly tools to prove what I have just said in proper academic fashion. To justify my saying it I can only plead a kind of literary intuition working upon my fund of life-experience. But I hope that someday properly qualified scholars will look into this matter of Uncle Josephus, and I am confident that, when they do, their findings will bear me out. Meanwhile, I am glad to think that Uncle Josephus lived long enough to see himself confirmed and vindicated in all that he did and sought to do.

Well, almost. It is a necessity of his myth pattern that a genuine culture hero be damned in his lifetime and canonized after his death. On December 2, 1963, at Bath, Maine, not very far up the coast from Newport, Rhode Island, the Navy's newest guided missile frigate was launched. A few days earlier, with all the solemn ceremonies traditional to such occasions, it had been christened the U.S.S. *Josephus Daniels*. Therewith the admirals finally completed the myth pattern. And that puts the capstone upon the story of Uncle Josephus.

❧ PART II

Insights of the Writer

From a speech given at East Carolina College, Greenville, N. C., March, 1963

On Creative Energy

~~ A FEW days ago I called a man in New York on long distance, and he was not in. The operator in Durham gave my telephone number to the secretary in New York so that she could call back when the man returned. I have one of the new numbered exchanges, but in New York they still have named exchanges.

"Please repeat the exchange," said Miss New York.

"It's nine-six-eight," said Miss Durham. She pronounced it *nahn*-six-eight.

"Is that Nancy-Kate?" Miss New York asked doubtfully.

"No! Nahn-six-eight!" said Miss Durham. *Stupid!* her voice implied.

From their voices, my writer's imagination knew at once that both were young and pretty girls. I listened with delight. The voices grew more impatient.

"Spell it. Won't you *please* spell it?" Miss New York pleaded.

"You *cain't* spell it! It's *numbers!*" Miss Durham said.

"I don't want the number. I already have the number," Miss New York said crisply. "Just please give me the exchange, will you, *please?*"

"Like I told you. Nahn-six-eight!"

"Nancy-Kate. Now is it *really* Nancy-Kate?"

"Listen! *Nahn!*" Miss Durham said desperately. "One-two-three-four-five-six-seven-eight-*NAHN!*"

"Nine? Are you saying *ni-yeen?*"

"Yes! *Nahn-six-eight!*"

"Nine-six-eight. Oh! It's a *numbered* exchange!" *Why didn't you tell me?* her voice implied.

For a moment I heard the distant rumble of the guns at Sumter. Then both girls giggled.

In setting out to make the particular statement about creative energy that I wish to impart here, I know that I face a barrier to understanding more formidable than the Mason-Dixon Line. It is the barrier between youth and age, for these remarks are addressed primarily to young men and women who are not yet twenty-one years old. What follows is an experiment in communication.

Everyone knows that creative energy is what produces art. Fewer know that it must power all significant work in science and in every scholarly pursuit. Not nearly enough people understand that it can also power every aspect of daily living and make the difference between dispirited boredom and a life that is vividly exciting regardless of external circumstances. My thesis is that we all begin life with a vast fund of creative energy and lose it along the way at rates which vary between individuals, so that among mature adults there is a far greater disparity than among children. My concern is to advise you, as college students, how best to retain as much as you can of your creative energy during the crucial period you have now entered, in which, in the normal course of things, so much of it is irrecoverably lost.

The problem and its solution are stated very well in Wordsworth's "Intimations" ode. I hope a good many of you have already read it with a certain puzzled interest, knowing its repute as great poetry, and yet in all honesty finding it incomprehensible and dull. I wish to translate Wordsworth's ode into contemporary terms and concepts and also to go somewhat beyond it, as our culture has gone far beyond what it was in Wordsworth's day. The ode embodies a subtle, elusive idea that cannot be bought over the counter or handed about like a package. It is more like

catching a bird in flight, and, if you are to stay with me, you must be prepared to fly a bit yourselves.

What Wordsworth chose to treat as different modes of being we can handle more easily nowadays with the concept of creative energy. There is still going on in all aspects of our culture a long-term shift from the statics of form to the dynamics of process, and the notion of energy is more familiar to us than it was to Wordsworth. We have a number of schools of dynamic psychology busily disagreeing about how best to construct a unified field theory of the human spirit. Their jargon is at least as confusing as and much less pleasant to the ear than Wordsworth's poetic phrases. In this talk I will avoid the jargon.

I will instead begin by defining creative energy simply by pointing at it in such a way that you can all identify it with something in your own direct experience. While it is possible and most fascinating to infer the operation of creative energy in very young infants, I am going to point to a later manifestation of it, one recoverable through memory in recognizable terms.

When I was eight or nine years old I read a story about cavemen, and one afternoon I went out to hunt a bear. I was going to bring him home to my cave as food for my parents and brothers, and I meant to make his pelt into a robe for myself. It did not bother me that my cave was a conventional house and that my forest was a desert expanse of sagebrush and lava rock where no bear had ever lived. My spear was a long wooden lath on which I had whittled a point. I set forth filled with pleasant excitement.

It was a hot afternoon, with the sky perfectly clear and the world flooded with light. The air was filled with a spicy sagebrush smell and the buzzing of locusts. Yet I went along in mounting excitement with the sense of a cool, shadowy forest all about me, and occasional sunny glades. I went somewhat further from home than I was accustomed to go in play, up a slight rise in the land, and finally, with a thrill of fearful delight, I came upon my bear.

He looked something like a rock, crusted with gray-green lichens and partially screened by clumps of sagebrush. I had been that far a few times before and I knew that he was a rock, but I did not know it so certainly that he could not also serve as a bear. *Safely* serve me as a bear, if you will dare to know what I mean. Down I went on hands and knees, heart thumping, spear gripped in my right hand, and I began to stalk him.

I was perhaps twenty feet away when his rump and haunch heaved slowly. The locusts stopped buzzing. I froze, breathless, with a watery thrill of weakness down my legs. The bear did not know yet that I was there. I could still creep away. Instead, I waited dry-mouthed until I recovered the marginal knowledge that he was also a rock. Then, with both knowings held in precarious balance, I resumed my stalking.

The outline of his haunch became plainer. I could see his flank heave with slow breathing. A tension of fearful delight grew in me almost past bearing. The bear sensed my approach and reared shaggily up to loom and roar. In a kind of chaotic swirling away of everything, I rushed screaming at the bear, thrusting and hacking and beating my lath to a splintered stump, until I had restored the set shape of things. I had slain the bearness of him and I had restored the rockness.

I had made him a rock for good and all. I stood there panting and trembling, and I knew that I could never hunt him again. But I would always have a friendship with him; he had become a place for me, which I could revisit with pleasure. There were still plenty of other rocks for me to hunt.

That experience is my own fundamental definition of creative energy. A good place for each of you to look for his personal definition might be in the area of night fears and fancies, because after dark the set shape of things has less power either to protect or to command us. If, as you search, you find yourself becoming uneasy and inclined to scoff, that is only to be expected. I say it sadly. I hope you will not let it defeat you.

It is to be expected because you are still too close to your child-hood, and all the shaping forces of our culture impel you to put away childish things. The world of childhood can be acutely disturbing to an older mind. Our primary defense is first to for-get it and then to insist that it never was because we cannot our-selves remember it. Wordsworth notes that often on his way to school he would have to grasp at a wall or a tree to make the physical world around him retain its set and proper shape. He found it terrifying.

Consider that for a moment in imagination. What would it be like to see the external physical reality all around you begin to shimmer and shift and sway like figures painted on a curtain? To see a cypress tree become a great roaring green flame? Who of us would not be terrified? Yet to a little child, who has not yet created for himself a stable and independent physical world, that is how it seems. It is no threat to him, because that is just how things are and they are pretty wonderful. The more surely he gains a stable physical world, the more of the fearful wonder he loses. As a boy, he can still recapture echoes of it in daring imaginary bear hunts. In full maturity, he may sometimes go at great expense to East Africa to shoot real lions. That is a very paltry substitute.

Wordsworth was understandably terrified. We all carry at vary-ing depths beneath our conscious memory that archaic, primor-dial terror. The inclination to scoff is a safeguard against its overwhelming re-emergence. It is a necessary safeguard. But, Wordsworth goes on, "In later periods of life I have deplored, as we all have reason to do, a subjugation of the opposite sort." I hope in these remarks to help those who can stay with me to avoid too complete and crushing a subjugation of that opposite sort.

You are moving now through a transition zone. "Shades of the prison house begin to close upon the growing boy." That has already happened to you. "The youth. . ./By the vision splendid/ Is on his way attended." That is where you are now. It is a great irony that you will not be able to appreciate the full splendor of

it until you have lost it, until "At length the Man perceives it die away/And fade into the light of common day."

That is where you are going, into the light of common day. What you will find it like when you get there will depend in part upon how much of your original stock of creative energy you will have succeeded in bringing through with you to be, in Wordsworth's phrase, the master light of all your seeing. And now, as I have called upon your memory to re-experience childhood, I would like to lead your imagination as far as it will reach toward an anticipation of your intellectual maturity.

To you now, physical reality is independent and mostly dead. It is no longer possible to turn a rock into a bear. It is not easy even to be friends with a rock in his essential rockness. But, just as the children you once were had to explore and to relate themselves to a wonderfully living, changing, unmanageable world of sticks and stones and bushes, so the youths you now are must explore and relate themselves to an equally fearful and wonderful world of ideas. No doubt you often find it confusing and difficult. Perhaps the idea you think you have grasped turns out not to be the idea your instructor thinks he has tossed at you. To you, ideas are still more like birds in flight, with a life and a will of their own, than they are like baseballs. In your thought-world you feel the "Blank misgivings of a Creature/Moving about in worlds not realized." Something of the same process which you have already gone through in your relation to the physical world must also take place in your relation to the world of ideas. It must take on for you a certain public stability and reality which is roughly the same for everyone. You are going to be very powerfully tempted to make it a small and, as far as possible, an unchanging world.

If, however, you let the process go too far, it can practically destroy that life of the mind which you now have in almost unimpaired vigor. There will be no more play and exploring. It will not be possible to go bear-hunting among ideas. Then the

thought-world is more of a prison house than a refuge, a narrow world of a few ideas, safe because they are fixed and solid as rocks. I do not mean that a man in that state no longer thinks. He can send his attention skipping as nimbly as ever among his stock of ideas. Just so can all of you still run and shout among the rocks and bushes if you like, but you know you are not doing the same thing as little children. The man I am describing can think, all right, but he can no longer think *creatively*. Nor is his state any bar to material prosperity. I think there are many men of power and affluence who are as frightened of an idea threatening to change shape as they would be of a rock changing into a bear. They are extreme cases of that subjugation of the opposite sort. For them the salt has lost its savor, and it is most merciful when the savor is lost so completely that not even an aching memory of it remains.

I will assume that no one who has come thus far with me wishes to end in that state, even if it means foregoing a certain measure of power and affluence. And I must warn you that our culture will move you by insensible degrees steadily in that direction, unless you resist it intelligently. Wordsworth's prognosis holds true for you all:

> Full soon thy Soul shall have her earthly freight
> And custom lie upon thee with a weight
> Heavy as frost and deep almost as life.

Here I am really extrapolating from the ode. The relative numbing of imagination had not gone so far in Wordsworth's day, when grown men and women could still find in traditional fairy tales the kind of delight that only quite young children can find in them in our time. Yet the experience is still the same, and we can still learn from Wordsworth.

We can learn that intellectual manhood does not come as suddenly or as early as we may have supposed. I know of no infallible

way to determine when it has come, but I can describe the particular signal by which I first discovered it in myself.

It was about midway through World War II, and I was on a ship in the South Pacific. I had charge of the watch in the engine room, in the sleepy hours after midnight, with nothing to do but walk around glancing at gauges and thermometers and listening to the steady hum of the turbines. It was my habit at such times to repeat poetry to myself, my favorite poems, of which I had many. I was just experiencing the music and pleasure of them without thought, the way another man might whistle a tune as he worked. I always had with me a pocket anthology of poetry, and I would sometimes read a poem which I did not have by heart. That night I read Wordsworth's "Intimations" ode. I had read it often before, with a certain puzzled interest, but I had never been able to make it *be poetry* for me. That night, suddenly and powerfully, it became poetry for me. It became magnificent poetry. "To me alone there came a thought of grief . . . But there's a Tree, of many, one . . ." I repeated, and the words dripped wonder. "Fallings from us, vanishings," I marveled aloud. The ode had become a poem not only of feeling and sense-imagery but also of ideas. It was my first clear signal that I was verging into what Wordsworth calls "the years that bring the philosophic mind."

If you will read and study it now, perhaps the ode can also serve some of you as an indicator. It cannot be magnificent poetry for you now because it is a memory of lost youth, and you are still immersed in youth. One cannot remember the present until it has become the past. But if in your thirties you still find the ode incomprehensible and boring to read all the way through, the chances are that you will have lost not only your youth but also the ability to remember it. You will have paid for intellectual manhood a far greater tax on your creative energy than was really necessary.

I was just past thirty when the ode became true poetry for me.

Wordsworth was thirty-three when he began it, and then he wrote only the first four stanzas. In them you can see him trying to resolve his "thought of grief," and you can see him fail. His fourth stanza ends with the same sad question:

Whither is fled the visionary gleam?
Where is it now, the glory and the dream?

Three years later Wordsworth answered himself in the final seven stanzas of the completed ode. It concerns us here mainly to note that he found a way to recover the glory and the dream and that he did it by taking hold of the stable and rocklike idea of Christian Immortality and putting it through some transformations. He alarmed certain good and pious persons who feared that he was changing their familiar rock into a strange one. He sought to reassure them by saying that he was only playing with poetic possibilities, thereby implying that their rock might not be as rocklike as they had thought it to be, and no doubt alarming them still more. It is in that notion of playing with poetic possibilities that we can find one clue to what we are seeking.

We must accept it as a sad fact that, after childhood, rocks will refuse to become bears for us. We can no longer play with sticks and stones as once we did. But that same lumpish, inert petrifaction does not ever have to happen to our world of ideas unless we, unwittingly, permit it to happen. It will not happen if we succeed in carrying over with us into the world of ideas enough of the shaping power of our imaginations which we first learned to use on the physical world around us. If we do that, we recover the glory and the dream. We can, if we like, again play directly with sticks and stones, but now as architects and builders.

The question is how, precisely how, are young persons like yourselves to carry over into your world of ideas as much as possible of the creative energy of childhood. I have no certain answer. But I believe that by a lucky chance I came through that

transition without a crippling loss, and all that I have learned up to this point in my life suggests some tentative answers. To them I now turn.

Most important, never stop using your creative energy. The more lavishly you pour it forth, the more abundantly will it always remain at your command. Do not hold back and seek anxiously for some worthy field on which to expend your energy. That is being miserly. It is in the nature of creative energy that the misers lose it all and only the spendthrifts retain it. Make the whole world of ideas your field. Regard each new idea you meet with a friendly or hostile interest, but never with indifference. Whenever you turn your back on an idea you close a door in your mind, and you may never again get it open.

Find your personal poet and make him part of yourself. Do not take him from anyone, no matter how august his authority; search and find your poet for yourself. He is likely not to be someone called great—for me at your age he was Kipling—but if you can meet him honestly and directly, without any screen of critical evaluation, he can let you into the world of poetic thought. That world is the least petrified of all. Once you are fairly inside it, by however humble an entrance, you cannot be wholly lost. From inside it you will go on making more poets and their poetry part of yourself without conscious volition, like something that grows of itself. From inside it you can approach the real giants, Milton and Shakespeare and Chaucer, and make them part of yourself in a way not possible by an approach from outside. It is the difference between *living* the poetry and just talking about it, however learnedly one may learn in time to talk.

I believe that what kept my mind alive and my fund of creative energy intact through all my years aboard ship was, more than anything else, my devotion to English poetry.

Make the same kind of entrance into the world of music and the plastic arts. Here I am in no position to speak with authority. In my day there was no art or music aboard warships, and they

were not something a man could bring aboard for himself, like a pocket anthology of poetry. But I passed my youth largely in China and Japan, where art is mingled intimately with all of daily living, and I made my entrance into that world through ways so diffuse and humble that I did not even know that I was in it. Only when I returned at last to the United States and missed it as a part of life did I learn to look for it in the special buildings set apart by our culture for such purposes. But just as with poetry, I think it is more conservative of creative energy if one learns to experience all art without self-conscious awareness, directly and wordlessly, before trying too hard to learn to talk about it.

Try to understand your years in college as a staking-out of the world of ideas in which you will live the rest of your life. Make it a wide one. In the world of real estate some men must inevitably be poor and narrowly restricted. Every man may claim for himself as much as he wishes of the world of ideas. Make each course you take an outpost of the imagination to hold for you some region of wonder for exploration later in your life. Claim more such regions now than you can possibly exhaust in ten lifetimes. Build yourself outposts in as many as possible of the sciences and furnish them with the beauty and wonder of art. The more weirdly outflung and roundabout your boundaries may seem to more conventional minds, the more richly wonderful will be the world you are claiming for yourself. Claim it now, and claim prodigally. Only so can you carry with you into that world an abundance of the creative energy which you must otherwise lose.

Understand each course you take as an investment of your creative energy, which thus will still be yours to draw upon in later years. The way to make it an investment rather than a tax or a purchase price lies in the attitude in which you approach it. The course will embody a set of ideas. Address yourself directly to those ideas. Push to one side as much as you can all thought of pleasing your parents or professors with high grades. Do not for

a moment think how you will someday use those ideas to make
money. All of that poisons the living relationship you will be
seeking. Simply become curious and explore those ideas in the
very same way a little child will explore first the house and then
the yard when his family moves to a new location. Do not expect
to grasp them at once and as concretely as so many rocks, although
the examination system will often seem to expect that of you.
Hope rather that you never grasp them in full concreteness. You
may often feel a certain baffled distress. That will be Wordsworth's "Blank misgivings of a Creature/Moving about in worlds
not realized." In years to come, if you can retain it, it will be a
source of great joy to you. If your grasp of an idea differs from
that of your professor, do not assume instantly that you are
wrong. Ideas are not rocks, and you may both be right. Argue it
in class and after class, and you may teach your teacher something.
If he is at all worthy of his vocation, he will love you for it. Even
one such experience in a course is a more genuine token of education than an A on the final exam. It is your assurance that you
have indeed invested there a portion of your creative energy, to
go on working autonomously and drawing interest against the
time that you will pass that way again.

In every term paper you write strive to tell the professor something about the course material which you suspect he has not yet
learned for himself. Give him *your* thoughts, gained by your own
exploration of the ideas, instead of just reflecting his thoughts.

You will meet certain invincibly dull and boring courses to
which you simply cannot imagine relating yourself in the manner
I have just described. I insist that you can. If you cannot kindle
a curiosity about its set of ideas, then explore them vindictively.
Go after them in order to revenge yourself by making fun of
them, by transforming them ludicrously in your term papers, by
seeking to deny their valid existence as ideas. If you provoke
them enough, they will defend themselves, and you will become
creatively engaged with them, which is what you must achieve
in every course if it is to be an investment of, rather than a tax

upon, your creative energy. Do not demand of all ideas that they must please or divert you; claim those that shock and frighten you as well. The world of the mind would be a pretty dull place if it were only one great flowery meadow; build yourself also cliffs and chasms, tawny deserts and polar wastes.

I can almost guarantee that one attitude or the other will take you creatively through the most dull and difficult of courses. Simply persist in trying to relate yourself directly to the set of ideas, and one or the other attitude will spring up within you. But you must persist, to the point of psychic discomfort. You must be like the man who dropped a nickel into a pond and threw a dollar after it in order to make it worth his while to recover both. Throw in your dollar and your wristwatch and your sweetheart and whatever else it may take to get you in there too. You must get in there, somehow creatively engaged with those ideas.

Another way of putting it is that you must begin now, while you still can, to play with ideas in precisely the way that children play with sticks and stones. Never stop playing with ideas as long as you live. Never grant to any idea the independent, unchanging, thing-in-itself existence which you have been forced to grant to rocks. Never grant to any professor the intellectual authority to make ideas into rocks for you. Those who do grant it, who indeed by their passive disengagement from ideas insistently demand it, in effect turn a university into a factory. They ride through it on an assembly line, and when they tumble off the end they will run, all right, but someone who has kept his creative imagination is going to have to drive them. That man will be a product of the living university of students and teachers jointly and creatively engaged with living ideas, *playing* with ideas. Insist on being one of the latter. So in the realm of thought you may remain young indefinitely, where another man, endowed by nature no less well than you, may be senile at thirty.

It will be said that you must live predictably and responsibly. That is true. But in the realm of thought never acknowledge any

master. In the realm of thought wear custom like a decent garment, but never let it come to lie upon you heavy as frost and deep almost as life. Then, when you are alone or in congenial company, you can cast it off and go adventuring. Men all around you will be living in stony thought-worlds sometimes sculptured grandly into Grecian architectural forms. Visit them there, for they are often good men. Do not disturb them with your freedom, for that would not be good manners. But if you feel your garment of custom beginning to cleave to your flesh, if you can detect a certain stoniness creeping about your ankles, make your excuses politely and get out fast.

It will be said that you must specialize rather narrowly in order to have a successful career. That also is true. But so mark out your private thought-world that you can at will bring to your specialty the resources of whole continents. What you will bring will be not so much a jumble of bits of knowledge as it will be a large and free and flexible habit of thought, that priceless ability to *play like children with ideas.* With it you can find new approaches to old problems and roundabout ways to valuable insights not available to your more stony competitors. For the sake of that advantage, in this crucial period of your lives take H. G. Wells as a kind of model. Of him it was said disparagingly that, while he was indeed a mile wide, he was only a foot deep. That is preferable to being a mile deep and only a foot wide, if one cannot have it both ways, because a mile will span a great many one-foot channels. I believe, however, that one can have it both ways if he chooses wisely and in time. Run widely now, in youth and early manhood, and you will retain sufficient volume to cut many deep channels later in life. But if you settle for a one-foot channel now, you will be trapped in that slot forever.

Up to this point I have been talking to you in terms of your individual self-interest. There is another aspect of this subject on which I wish to touch briefly before concluding.

Our private thought-worlds must all take account of one another and combine into the common thought-world of our culture. The private thought-worlds range by minute gradations between extremes of stony immutability and surrealistic freedom. The proportions in which they combine determine for our common thought-world something we may call an index of plasticity. I mean by that a relative ability to change and adapt in order to relieve stress rather than to shatter into stony fragments when the stress becomes too great to resist any longer. I believe that the plasticity index of our culture is dangerously low. It can only be raised by mixing into the culture new minds more free and more abundantly supplied with creative energy to replace the stony old ones which are dying off.

It happens that some regions of our culture are more free and plastic than others. Those of you who manage to retain a large share of your creative energy will be tempted to move into those free areas and to confine yourselves there. By so doing you will be of little help in raising our over-all index of plasticity. You may rather, by helping to increase the rate of change in those areas, work to increase the stress which gravely threatens the more stony parts of our culture.

One free region is art. An artist is still free to see the bear-quality in a black rock and to take his sculptor's tools and liberate the bear. But it is ominous that not many artists are doing anything like that these days; what they seem to see in all they look at is chaos and old night. Another free region is science. By playing with ideas, the scientists have learned how to abstract from black rocks a certain metal which, assembled in the critical quantities already on hand, can destroy all life on our planet.

So, to conclude, there is a certain standpoint of thought from which I can tell you honestly that whether and in what proportions you can come through these college years with your creative energy undiminished may well determine whether or not our culture is to survive. You will not help much if you hide your-

selves away in science and art. What you must do is diffuse in your own persons the freedom of science and art, the incomparably precious ability to *play like children with ideas,* through the other and stonier parts of our common thought-world. If just enough of you can do that to slightly leaven the lump, I think we may all be saved.

From an article in The Writer, *there titled "Creative Energy and Fiction Writing,"* LXXVI, No. 6 (June, 1963). *Copyright © 1963 by The Writer, Inc.*

On Becoming a Writer

∾ THIS brief article is a collective answer to many letters to which I have not had time to give individually the attention they deserve. It is also addressed to all those who are not full-time, professional, free-lance writers and who wish to be.

To write anything, and in particular to write fiction, you must expend creative energy. We all have a natural fund of creative energy, and we cannot be altogether happy unless we are able to release it in full. Children do so in play. Writing fiction is a kind of grown-up make-believe, but it is very far from being child's play. I am concerned that many of you seem unconsciously so to understand it.

For adults, creative outlets are many and widely varied. How sure are you that writing fiction is the only one for you? Since infancy you have been developing verbal skills. You know how to write letters. Therefore it may seem easier to you to seek a creative outlet in writing than in composing music or in carving marble. But how do you know that you are not mistaking the mere convenience of writing for a genuine vocation to write?

Take the trouble to learn the meaning of *vocation*, not from a dictionary but from a priest or minister. Study Joyce's *Portrait of the Artist as a Young Man*. It has been said that one who has a vocation to write does not have to wonder about it. If you have any doubt about your own, I can suggest a reliable way to test it.

Try to deny it. Flee it, as Jonah fled the command of God. Make your voyage to Tarshish a search for alternate creative out-

lets. If you really arrive at Tarshish, I know writers who will consider you fortunate.

I know a woman who averages one very fine short story a year. Her life has been a stormy voyage of successive marriages wrecked upon rocks and shoals. At times she feels an urge to cook something special. For days she will turn out elaborate meals with fancy desserts, and her family will prize her above rubies. If when the urge comes, however, she instead feeds them canned beans and lets the house go and sits resolutely at her typewriter, she will sooner or later write a very good short story.

There is a lesson in her life. I suspect she has reached Tarshish repeatedly and has refused to go ashore. It has not made her happy.

Do not lightly equate public notice and acclaim with personal satisfaction. I wish all girls and women who have come this far with me would make a note to study or restudy the character of Mrs. Ramsay in *To the Lighthouse*. Mrs. Ramsay's creative outlet was people. She composed dinner parties. She orchestrated human lives. For the increasing lack of women like Mrs. Ramsay our world is becoming an emotional junkyard. I would prefer to be friend and familiar to Mrs. Ramsay than to Virginia Woolf, who created her. So too, I suspect, would Virginia Woolf have preferred. Virginia Woolf had an undeniable vocation to write. I doubt it ever made her very happy.

Seven years ago, when I set out to write, I was newly married and living in a shabby old house. Some days I wrote and some days I did painting and tiling and carpentry. I began to notice the same subjective pattern and quality in both kinds of work. There were the same stages of planning, the same curve of mounting excitement in the execution. At some deep level in me redoing a room and writing a short story were the same activity.

In the same proportion as my writing gained in power, my home-workshopping dwindled. My tools are rusting now. Most days, I will not so much as drive a nail to hang a picture.

We all have by nature a fund of creative energy. I wish people

would not assume so readily that it can be released only through channels labeled *art*. It can be released in almost any human activity, if the effort is made. It can be spread evenly through all the functions of living to build what I consider a full and beautiful life. I think a simple life lived in harmony with the people around one is as much a work of art as a book or painting. Certainly it can be made richer with books and paintings and music, as long as they are kept creatively harmonious with the whole. And I think anyone who would voluntarily forego such a life is near to being mad.

Too many of you who haunt creative writing classes and writers' conferences could approximate such a life, and you are trying to avoid it. You think you wish to learn improved techniques of literary expression. What you are really after is the secret of writing. You will not learn it in a creative writing class. You might come nearer doing so in a creative reading class. You will not learn it from personal association with writers who have it. You will come nearer such men by reading their books creatively than you ever will by talking to them face to face.

The primary secret of writing, as I understand it, is the concentration of as much as possible of one's creative energy upon the work of writing. It is an ingathering and focusing, to the relative impoverishment of other areas of life, and it is never done by an act of will. It comes as an ambivalent visitation, and he to whom it comes will be wretchedly unhappy until he finds an adequate outlet for it. That is what I mean by having a vocation.

The work tends to engulf the whole of such a man's creative energy. At peak flow his social life almost vanishes. He wishes it would. He will sit when he must in the company of his blood brothers and dearest friends, grimly enduring and resenting them. All who demand his time and attention seem to him persons from Porlock intent on destroying his work. For the sake of his work, helplessly, he will deny and reject them all. In order to relate through his writing to all humanity he must reject all particular human beings, including himself as such. He will feel

painful guilt for it; he may fear that he is becoming spiritually
malformed into a monster; but he will do it anyway. He will wish
he could flee to a remote cabin or hide among an alien population and often enough finds he must.

I have described an extreme case. Mercifully, when the work
is done, the man resumes a semblance of normal humanity. Many
good writers do not while working contract their personal life
so nearly to the vanishing point. Neither do they write with all
the power of which they are potentially capable, and most of
them know it. They are often unhappily caught in a tug-of-war
between their work and the other obligations of their life.

Therefore, to anyone who is already enmeshed in a web of
human relationships and who wishes also to become a professional writer of fiction, I say *stop trying*. Try instead to expend
your excess creative energy in daily living. There are cooking
and gardening and carpentry and sewing and a host of other pur-
suits, not least of which is the creative guidance of human per-
sonalities taking shape in children. Try to feel it not as drudgery
but as an opportunity for imagination. Try to lavish the whole
of your creative energy on it and not meanly and guiltily pinch
away all that you can to expend on something you think is art.
You will never pinch away enough to do you any good. And for
the fortunate ones, living in itself can be an art.

If you are not one of the fortunate ones, if you cannot get
ashore at Tarshish, you will soon enough know it. But do not
without a struggle abandon that first line of defense. I spent
eighteen years trying to find a creative outlet in marine engineering. I should have given up after four years. Yet those who have
not tried it might be surprised to learn how much creative energy can be expended on machinery. I knew many good men for
whom it was an adequate outlet, and I envied them. Their lives
have been happier than mine.

For the less fortunate there is a second line of defense. Write,
but write with a limited objective. Write letters. Keep a journal.

If you must publish, write for newspapers or house organs or trade journals. Never mind that some will say it is not art. If you can make it an adequate outlet for your excess creative energy, you thereby make it art in terms of your own life. Some of the best writing I read these days is on the editorial pages of newspapers. If you have been honestly forced to the second line, you will have no problem about learning to write. You will learn almost without effort.

For me the second line was newspaper writing. I learned it so quickly it almost seemed as if I had always known it. Yet to the end I would spend hours of my supposedly free time at night rewriting and polishing a single editorial or feature story. I had found for my creative energy a more adequate outlet than I had ever had before. Yet very soon the ingathering process concentrated my energy still more, and the outlet was no longer sufficient. There were good men in my office for whom it was sufficient, and they are still newspapermen. Their lives also have been happier than mine.

I could not bring myself to change my Navy rating from machinist's mate to journalist. When the Korean War obliged me to serve an extra two years, I went back to sea in the engine room of a destroyer. Those came near being the two most miserable years of my life. When I finished them, I fell back on the third line of defense.

The third line of defense is a forlorn hope. It lies on the yonder side of what is generally agreed to be art. I do not know about Pure Art. I am more comfortable thinking in terms of gradually increasing artistry in the use of verbal skills which we all begin learning in childhood. Any sharp division is likely to be arbitrary. Yet there is a distinct difference on the third line. I prefer to think of it as a sudden freeing of the imagination from external authority.

And now I have said all I can that may be of help and comfort to you who are on the third line without having been forcibly

dislodged from the first two lines. Go back and make the fight. I wish you luck. Return here only because you know you must and not because you think you want to.

Those who have been forced back to the third line do not write me the kind of letters I have been trying to answer here. They know they are never going to make it to Tarshish. They can prolong the voyage; they can cling to a lodgment on the third line possibly all their lives; but they will never be truly happy. However hidden, even from ourselves, a something haunts us. We reread *Moby Dick* and feel uneasily, without understanding a bit of it, that the last portion of Father Mapple's sermon is aimed at us. Darkly deep behind shielding veils of inwardness there is a place where we are always going to despise ourselves until we find the courage to leave soundings and put to sea in our personal *Pequods*.

But that is a subject for a different letter.

From a speech at the annual meeting of the Friends of the Chapel Hill Public Library, Chapel Hill, N. C., May 12, 1964

The Glory and the Dream

WHEN I first heard that Chapel Hill was to have a public library, I thought it a fine idea—a most excellent undertaking—and I was all for it. I have never wavered in that conviction. Yet, working through the resources of the Wilson Library, my wife had all along been getting for me almost any book I wanted, and I felt no personal need of a public library in Chapel Hill. Why, then, should I have been so pleased about having one? It was not wholly sentiment. It was no dogmatic all-books-are-good major premise. It was more than sympathy with people who did not happen to have a professional librarian in the family. I had a sense of the direction in which the answer lay, and when I found the moon athwart that path, I could probably have thrust it aside in a brisk no-nonsense manner and gone on soberly to my goal. But since Robert Graves long ago taught me to defer to the moon, and since the moon obviously wished to be included, I did not do so. All the signs, which I have half-learned to read by now, pointed to a genuine tie between the moon and the Chapel Hill Public Library. I thought it might be of some interest and amusement to discover it.

First I tried linking the two in various titles, like shuffling a set of cards. Often a seemingly chance combination will ring a bell. No bells rang for me, however. The most euphonious title I came up with, "Lunatics and Libraries," was obviously the least suitable. Well then, I thought, I will just for the moment stop thinking about libraries altogether and simply think about the moon.

We hear much talk these days about men going to the moon. I remember a time when we could run the whole country for about what we now spend annually on preparing to send a man to the moon. Through all the talk are woven various reasons for the moon project. The scientists wish to increase the store of human knowledge. Some of the military people would be pleased to have a missile base on the moon. The TV people like the spectacular visual and sound effects. The space effort generates some hefty payrolls in a number of congressional districts. Many of us simply hope to beat the Russians to it in order to enhance our national prestige within the world community. No doubt among the moon-shooters there are a few stern, bronzed men who will murmur: "Because it's there."

Cliché or no, I suspect those men are nearest to having the right of it. But I must find a less bearded and taciturn way of saying it, one which will also implicate the Chapel Hill Public Library in our national moon-aspirations. New ideas are often first expressed by poets, although they may not be understood until several generations later. So I turn my mind to the English poets.

They afford no immediate insights. Mooning restlessly about the house, I reflect that in English poetry the moon is always feminine. She is an "orbèd maiden, with white fire laden." Such a myth-conception, although true enough, can never be considered *there* in the sense of extended substance filling a region of space, as with the peak of a mountain. For the poets it is easier, both on themselves and on the taxpayers. They either worship from afar or by the power of their longing persuade the moon to come to them. The latter is not without its own kind of hazard, as Keats and "Endymion" will bear witness, but the poet pays all the forfeit.

Long ago in the West we began making a distinction between truth and poetry. Aristotle suspected all poets of being liars, gay deceivers of the soberly rational intellect. Plato would have none

of their disruptive influence in his eternally static ideal society. Our distinction between truth and poetry has until recently been not too apparent to most non-Western peoples.

In their minds the moon has been totally a myth-conception. In China he is an old man, and not always a wise old man, who ties young men and women together with an invisible thread, whereupon they are fated to marry each other. That suggests various motives for the Chinese to visit the moon, now that we have enforced upon them the knowledge that the moon is *there*. The Japanese moon is male also. He is consort to, and of rather small account within the household of, his more resplendent lady who rules by day. Yet he is thought to be a strong and handsome man armed with a golden sword and dwelling in a fine palace beside the River of Fifty Bells. Perhaps in Japan it will be the women, now emancipated and permitted to know that the moon is really *there*, who will move to put a woman upon the moon.

I find that an intriguing thought but unfortunately most remote from the Chapel Hill Public Library. I am about to strike off in another direction when a nursery rhyme, with a Japanese look about its eyes, dances into view.

> I saw an old woman go up in a basket
> Seventeen times as high as the moon.
> Where she was going I couldn't but ask it,
> For in her hand she carried a broom.
>
> "Where are you going, Old Woman?" quoth I.
> "To sweep the cobwebs out of the sky."

I know at once that she is an aspect of the Muse not yet copyrighted by Robert Graves. Sure enough, directly thereupon the cobwebs begin to clear away from my own vision.

I reflect that, although I must help pay for the American moon-voyaging, I am not myself likely to be asked to go along anytime soon. Yet I do not feel discriminated against because I have the distinct feeling that I have already been to the moon more times

88/NEW EYES FOR OLD

than I can count, surely. First impressions, they say, are always the most lasting, and I remember best my early moon-visits in the company of Jules Verne and H. G. Wells.

That does bring books into it, but in much too trivial a way to be what I seek. I know I have been put upon the trail of a more considerable thought. Very well then, I will follow it. It leads me into reflections upon the human imagination in general and in particular upon imaginary moon-voyages.

The human imagination can express itself in many forms, not all of them commonly thought of as Art. No human activity is utterly void of it, and I think a great scientist or political leader is as truly an artist as any great painter or poet. I often make use of a plausible way of thinking in which groups of people, through whom collectively a particular culture manifests itself, have thereby an unconscious collective mind which cannot help dreaming. Embedded within such groups, the artists—and I mean to include political leaders—serve as channels through which the collective dreams can be expressed in actions and forms accessible to conscious understanding. Maybe that is the function of the artist in any society. I have ranged widely enough through the mythology and literature of non-Western peoples to confirm for myself a discovery made long before me: that a remarkable similarity of pattern runs through it all. It leaves me with little doubt of the truth of an even older intuition expressed by Matthew Arnold in the line: *The same heart beats in every human breast.* Yet nearer the surface, although still deep, there is a distinction between the West and all of the others, and one indication of it is that only the West has a long, evolving tradition of imaginary moon-voyages. And here some unpretentious lines of Kipling jingle up:

> I have been given my charge to keep—
> Well have I kept the same!
> Playing with strife for the most of my life,
> But this is a different game.

I'll not fight against swords unseen,
Or spears that I cannot view—
Open the gate, he must enter in state,
'Tis the Dreamer whose dreams come true.

It is there, I think, that one form of collective dreaming has until recently been peculiarly Western. It is not a new thought, but I can't remember where I first met it, possibly right there in Kipling. Anyway, it has been defined as the ability to *dream concretely*, and the history of our moon-voyage dream most beautifully exemplifies it. If, over the past few centuries, the West has had any secret of success within the world community, that is probably it.

Well, it has been very nice having it, even if it is not a secret any longer, but one of the not-so-nice consequences of dreaming concretely is that we cannot evade moral responsibility for what we have chosen to dream. During World War II someone said of that great artist Adolf Hitler that he was a psychotic who hallucinated concretely. Hitler is dead now, but the mad fragments of his dream live on within us, as they were there before Hitler bodied them forth in a decade of history, and they may yet destroy us all.

I turn with relief from that uneasy thought back to the more innocuous moon. I must suppose that shaggy creatures looked up to it, perhaps drummed on their chests and howled to vent an otherwise inexpressible emotion, for millions of years before Eve ate the apple and plunged us all into the human condition. There followed the amassing of a rich heritage of myth-dreaming upon the moon. I think the first people to look upon the moon with the wild surmise that it was really *there*, like an island in the sea, were the Greeks. Only a fraction of Greek literature has come down to us, but included in it are two highly imaginative voyages to the moon.

Lucian of Samosata wrote them both, in the second century A.D. The motive he gave his hero, Menippus, on what may be the

very first such flight in the history of the human imagination, is still to my mind the very best one of all. Menippus was tired of wars and bitter wrangling, and he flew to the moon in order to get far enough away from the Earth to see it steadily and see it whole. What he saw appalled him. I hope that we or the Russians, whoever first establishes safe travel to the moon, will forthwith invite all Earth's heads of state up there for a summit conference.

Among the Greek city-states they could not achieve that degree of detachment in time; and, as we all know, the Greeks went under. Europe went back to myth-dreaming for a thousand years. After Lucian it was thirteen hundred years before another man wrote an account of an imaginary moon-voyage. The man was Ariosto, in Italy in 1532, and the reason he got away with it was that it was wildly, poetically imaginary. A full century after Ariosto the poet got away with it, Galileo the scientist had to recant in order to escape possible burning alive. He had stated as a fact, among other even more blasphemous notions, that the moon was really *there* and had mountains on it.

That was during the time when our forebears were discovering and making their own certain treasures of the Greek heritage which we northern forest-dwellers might not to this day have discovered for ourselves. They were learning how to become dreamers whose dreams come true. We all know what a splendid, centuries-long-enduring, ever-augmented outpouring of creative human energy was kindled by that touch of Promethean fire.

After Ariosto, imaginary moon-voyages come along regularly. In running down the list of them I note a curious trend: they are becoming more and more detailed and realistic, more concerned with getting there plausibly and less concerned with what they find upon arrival. Menippus simply straps on a pair of wings and flies up. Ariosto's man borrows Elijah's chariot. Like very small children at play, the authors just wave aside the physical barrier to their make-believe. But the parallel development of science keeps making that barrier less easy to wave aside. The writers respond with more ingenuity, and it is becoming some-

thing like a dialogue between the collective conscious and unconscious. The dream is growing up, becoming more and more concrete. When H. G. Wells goes to the moon in 1901, he is impeccably scientific about it except for one assumption. Even before he makes that assumption, scientists probably not known to him—Albert Einstein for one—are already moving to unriddle its active principle.

And now with the publication of Wells's novel a strange thing happens. Quite abruptly the moon-dream, as dream, begins to wane in quality and in literary repute. It becomes a theme for juvenile fiction only, then drops over for sporadic appearances in the pulp magazines.

Wells's novel, then, was the last of a distinguished lineage. Two years later a Russian scientist published the first book of a new lineage. His book was a completely serious engineering study of a moon-flight. He stated all the problems clearly and foresaw solutions to them all when current trends in existing technology should have advanced a few more decades. Oberth in Germany took up where the Russian left off. Werner von Braun and his associates grew up in the shadow of Oberth. The rest we know from reading our morning newspapers.

There, sketched in, we have the two-thousand-year life history of a collective human dream. It was passed from the Greeks to us like an Olympic torch and by us killed in the imminent achievement. Concrete dreams live in the not-yet. They are carried down the years through successive generations of living human imagination. It is fascinating to watch the moon-dream grow and evolve through a series of books which diffuse it ever more widely and circumstantially through each generation of new young minds. And by thus linking the moon with books I have established at least a tenuous sort of link between the moon and the Chapel Hill Public Library.

However, it is by no means as clear and meaningful as I would like it to be, so I must be off on still another random circuit round Robin Hood's barn. To guide me I see, hovering off at

the edge of vision, a pitiful, wizened face. It is Holden Caulfield, age sixteen and mourning for his lost youth. More lines from Kipling tug at my elbow.

> We have no heart for the fishing, we have no hand for the
>   oar—
> All that our fathers taught us of old pleases us now no
>   more.
> All that our own hearts bid us believe, we doubt where we
>   do not deny—
> There is no proof in the bread we eat, or rest in the toil
>   we ply.

The moon-dream is dead, all right, honorably and properly dead in the imminent achievement of it, but what of the other concrete human dreams for whose futility the metaphor *reaching for the moon* once served? Why should not the actual obtaining of the physical moon powerfully regalvanize the pursuit of those other and metaphorical moons? For some while we have been hearing a dismal chorus asking what has happened to the American Dream. From our artists we receive ever more sad and horrifying answers. The American Dream, our collective unconscious tells us through Henry Miller, has become an air-conditioned nightmare. What Edward Albee is calling it I shudder even to think.

I happen to believe that the American Dream is still most powerfully alive. I don't think a people can kill a dream like that except by making it come true. If they try hard enough to kill it in some other way, it will turn into a monster and kill them. I think the American Dream still lives in the books on the shelves of almost any library, but something is hampering its transmission through the books into the living imaginations of young Americans. I tend to understand that as a kind of decay of the imagination that has latterly come over us. Either it is woodenly almost not there at all or it is a tortured and writhing faculty,

expressing itself in bizarre and disturbing forms. Pretty clearly, all is not well within the Temple.

Yet I am as sure as can be that our children are still being born with as wholesome and exuberant imaginations as ever children had anywhere. I will wager there is not a three-year-old in Chapel Hill so far past his youth that he has any trouble imagining the cow jumping over the moon. In fact, if someone would just take him over there to the horizon where the moon is now rising, he would cheerfully undertake to jump over it himself or at least to climb aboard. Some years ago I read a news story of a small heroine of the human spirit, and I wish now that I had clipped and saved it. One fine evening in a small American town somewhere two frantic parents called the fire department to come and fetch their six-year-old daughter down out of a tree. The little girl was sixty feet up in the tree, and when the firemen ran a ladder up there and plucked her off it, she protested bitterly. Her badly shaken parents demanded of her what on Earth she had thought she was up to, and she replied calmly that she had been on her way to the moon. I glow with pride whenever I think of that little girl, who must be entering high school about now, and I hope she will not have to marry Holden Caulfield.

Here I come upon an old and well-beaten trail of mine which I might have reached more directly if I had not been moon-bemused into taking the long way round. To pay for my pleasure in that, I must now compress into a few sentences the results of a great deal of thinking.

How do societies *conserve* imagination? What institutional means have they to help individuals carry over into maturity some good part of their natural childhood endowment with that magic power? In preliterate societies it seems just to happen, mainly because the childhood imagination does not mature very much. The unlettered country folk of Wordsworth's day and place, grown men and women around the hearth of an evening, would retell to each other with pleasure the English fairy tales

that Holden Caulfield probably began rejecting as corny at the age of six. Wordsworth went among those folk to refresh his own poetic imagination. But somehow, if misused, the letter has power to maim the spirit. Wordsworth states the problem and his personal solution of it in his "Intimations" ode. How he achieved the philosophic mind we learn from his "Prelude."

There is no time to present evidence for what I wish to say next. There is no time to explore the presumed mechanics of how it happens. But sometimes still it does happen that a child moves onward to maturity carrying with him a very considerable part of his childhood imagination. One of the various ways that it can happen is by transfer to reading silently and alone the pleasure that all normal children take in hearing stories told or read aloud in company. I will sketch out what I believe to be the conditions under which it is most likely to happen.

The child has much unsupervised playtime. He can sometimes be alone if he wishes. He lives in a household where stories are told or read aloud and talked about afterward, so that the characters in them, Huck Finn or Penrod Schofield or whoever, seem to him almost like members of his family. In his home there is a varied selection of books, many too difficult for him, but all accessible to him at will. Near his home is a small public library or a neighborhood branch of a large one. In it all the books are in sight. He may handle them and look at them and linger with them deliciously before choosing for as long a time as he pleases. No one in particular will urge him to read books or praise him too extravagantly when he does so for his own pleasure. Hardly ever will anyone officiously thrust books upon him. Above all, no one will impress upon him reasons other than his own pleasure for the reading of books. I mean here specifically such reasons as may persuade him to think of books as scalps to hang at his belt or as objects to be piled in a heap and metaphorically stood upon so that he will stand taller in life than the other little boys who do not read.

Books which are primarily works of art can, in a mystical way,

function as persons. Possibly they cannot really function in any other way except as decor or doorstoppers. The boy will learn first of all to meet such books person-to-person, as friends, as ends in themselves and never as a means to some ulterior end of his own. Very early on he will understand without being able to say it in words that such books *enjoy being read* as much as he enjoys reading them. Then later in life no book, however technical and impersonal, however much a means to a scholarly end, can be wholly lifeless and alien to him. His very hands will have learned to love the feel of a book.

Here, having at last reached my point about the Chapel Hill Public Library, I will not labor it. I value and support our public library because it pleases me to have in our town a hostelry where books live as ends in themselves, for the mutual pleasure they can take and give, and where children can come and make friends with them before going on to the august Wilson Library behind its abstract barrier of the card catalog. Here also is a strategic place for an acknowledgment I should have made earlier. To study up the life history of the moon-dream I called upon Professor J. O. Bailey's excellent book *Pilgrims through Space and Time*. I read the book again with as much pleasure as I had years ago read it for the first time, and I was really asking and receiving help from an old friend.

The other conditions I propose for conserving imagination in a literate society are not so easily met. There are many, many homes with no books at all and no will to acquire any. The youngsters who need our public library most desperately are the ones stopped short on the path that leads to it. Governor Sanford has moved with vigor and bold imagination to break what he calls the *cycle of poverty* in our state. He sees at the root of material poverty a prior mental and cultural impoverishment the forestalling of which may solve much of the problem. That is akin to what I am calling conservation of imaginative power. But that carry-over into maturity of the ability to dream boldly and concretely is not a necessary consequence of a completed educa-

tion. It is the consequence of an inner, self-maintaining process which can assimilate itself to formal education. I think that process must be kindled quite early in life if the Promethean fire in that life is to burn at all strongly and clearly. One sure occasion on which it is kindled is when a child learns by himself to make friends *with* books before he is taught by his elders to make tools *of* them.

Therefore, now that President Johnson wishes to move on the national level to break that vicious circle of human potentiality stifled almost at birth in each generation, I hope some one of his advisers will remember a meek little by-the-way program of World War II. That was the Armed Services Editions of good books. They were utterly of the cheapest in physical being, costing probably two or three cents each to produce, but they were honest and friendly books, real books, utterly superior to the opulent and empty twenty-five-dollars-a-copy nonbooks which our publishers now bring out in shoals just prior to each Christmas season. Those little books were sown broadcast, like seed, through all the men in uniform. I think their juxtaposition with military boredom and depression gave many a young man a second chance to make friends with books long after the optimum time for doing so had seemingly passed him by. I believe that because of those little books quite a few young men went on to complete their educations under the G.I. Bill who might otherwise have fallen back into the cycle of poverty into which, some would say, it had pleased God to have them born.

I would like to see those little books revived and sent by couples and threes into all the impoverished households of the land, along with the rations of surplus food. It would not matter if in nine out of ten of those households the books were torn up to kindle cooking fires as long as in the tenth one, or even in the hundredth one, they chanced to be read and thereby served to kindle anew in some little girl or boy the Promethean fire that was otherwise doomed to flicker out. I would like to see those little books sown broadcast in the careless faith and manner of

old Johnny Appleseed. After a few years I would expect to see many a tall young life rising skyward from out the most unlikely weed-tangles.

I know, of course, all of the many reasons why such a program is as impossibly crack-brained a fancy as reaching for the moon. It could be done that other time only because it was a part of the war effort, and even then it was slighted and grudged by many who could not see how those little books might contribute to combat efficiency. It is a sad thought to ponder upon that we set hardly any limits to our collective generosity when it is a matter of destroying human lives somewhere overseas, but we tend to become very canny and reluctant when it is a matter of salvaging human lives here in our own country.

For some minutes now I have been orbiting around the Chapel Hill Public Library, but I have by no means abandoned that orbed maiden who powers Robert Graves and all true poets. I am not a poet myself, but in my thinking I make much use of poetry. All through this roundabout exercise of the imagination I have been using bits and pieces from the English poets, not always crediting them. They are part of the scaffolding which I have not had time to clear away. I believe with Shelley that the Promethean fire burns more brightly in the poets than in anyone else, wherefore I must reject much of contemporary poetry as being little more than howls and gobbles in the dark, and I believe with Arnold and Carlyle that the true poets are the nearest thing we have to prophets in these latter days. The lines that suggest themselves here are somber ones.

> Before a midnight breaks in storm
>   Or herded sea in wrath,
> Ye know what wavering gusts inform
>   The greater tempest's path?
>   Till the loosed wind
>   Drive all from mind
> Except Distress, which, so will prophets cry,
> O'ercame them, houseless, from the unhinting sky.

That was written in 1903. In his later years Kipling may have thought that he had been prophesying the first World War. I am not so sure that that was all he was prophesying. In his analytical biography of the moon-dream, Professor Bailey notes that sometimes the description of the moon-society serves as a commentary, generally satirical, upon Earthly society. That is a coloration taken from a parallel and equally old collective dream, also passed to us like an Olympic torch from Greeks long since gone under, but one which has not yet died by virtue of coming true. On the contrary, it is now more vigorously alive than ever. It is spreading like a conflagration of Promethean fire among all the peoples of Earth now waking up and becoming literate after millennia of myth-dreaming.

Professor Bailey follows convention and calls it the dream of Utopia. Because we have been so well-conditioned to dismiss that word as connoting a kind of foolish, idealistic reaching for the moon, I prefer to call it the dream of free men in a just society. I think that for a long time we Americans dreamed it more boldly and concretely than any other people on Earth. It is not possible for us to stop dreaming it. Trying to do so only turns it into a nightmare that comes and kneels upon our chests at midnight. We cannot stop dreaming it except by vanishing ourselves out of history or else by making it come true. And to the extent that we as a people try to pretend that we are as near to putting the capstone on a just society as we are to putting a man upon the moon, to that same extent are we benighted in error as surely as ever were the heathen in their blindness when the white man's cannon thundered down their gates.

Once the need of our land was said to be men to match its mountains. That does not take much of a man these days. Our mountains are all fitted up with escalators for the convenience of Holden Caulfield. Now we need more young men and women rising with unstifled imaginations from out the bitter strength of our land, able to make friends with the books that express the

dream and to infuse their lives into the dream and so stand forth to match our neighbors.

"Bliss was it in that dawn to be alive," Wordsworth said, recollecting in tranquillity the glory of the dream when it first suffused his own youthful imagination, "But to be young was very Heaven."

There is a necessary ambiguity in all true poetry. When we read a poem properly, we mix the truth of our islanded selves with the larger truth of the poem, and what we experience is a fusion of the two. Commonly it is a releasing and enlarging experience, and we are the better for it afterward. But it follows that the same poem can mean different things to different men, or to the same man at different periods of his life, and all of the things that it means are equally true. To the degree that what I have been saying has been conveyed through scraps of poetry— the scaffolding I have not had time to clear away—I cannot be sure of what I have actually said here to anyone except myself. I rather like that thought. It gives me at second hand something of the freedom of expression true poets must have if they are not to perish out of the land. Therefore I will conclude now with two more veiling scraps of poetry.

> I'd not give way for an Emperor,
> I'd hold my road for a King—
> To the Triple Crown I would not bow down—
> But this is a different thing.
> *I'll* not fight with the Herald of God
> (I know what his Master can do!)
> Open the gate, he must enter in state,
> 'Tis the Dreamer whose dreams come true.

The poetry I have been quoting is all of the easy, jingling sort with which children can quickly make friends. Poems are the finest sort of friends to make when one is young, and they will stay with a man all his life. They will comfort him in trouble,

and they will guide him in perplexity. I hope there is a lot of such easy, jingling poetry, from Mother Goose and William Blake right on through to Rudyard Kipling, living on the shelves of the Chapel Hill Public Library and waiting to make friends with the children. For, as Kipling said of some of his own friends in quite a different context:

In telegraphic sentences, half nodded to their friends,
They hint a matter's inwardness—and there the matter ends.

❧ PART III

A Book Emerges

From a speech at the Washington Post *Book and Author Luncheon, Washington, D.C., February 13, 1963*

The Fiction of History

❧ ONE of the questions that keep recurring in the mail I have been receiving since the publication of *Sand Pebbles* is: How true is the novel to the actual history of the times? Other letters, from businessmen and missionaries and gunboat sailors who lived through those times in Central China, congratulate me on how vividly I have recreated the period exactly as they remember it. Certain old sailors have even written me convinced that the *San Pablo* was really their old ship.

Offhand, the second group would seem to answer the first, but it is not that simple. What is involved is the relation of historical fiction to actual history. I am not going to draw any general conclusions. I mean to discuss this relationship solely in terms of the case history of the one historical novel I know most about.

In the case of *Sand Pebbles*, I knew the fiction before I knew the history. The book is not autobiographical. While the Chinese Revolution was going on I was a schoolboy in an isolated little desert town in Idaho, and I am quite sure I knew nothing about it. There was no radio. Our weekly newspaper printed only local news. All I can remember knowing about world affairs at that time was that the Finns were being good about paying their war debts and the French were being very difficult. I did not hear anything about the Chinese Revolution until I joined the Navy and went to duty in China.

Then I learned of it through the yarns of older sailors, who never called it a revolution. They gave it more the sense of a rebellion, as in Boxer Rebellion, and the phrase they most often used was "the troubles back in twenty-six and -seven." Through

the years I heard the same yarns told by different men, often with variations. They seldom claimed to have played a part in the event themselves, but I, as a listener, somehow felt they had. I felt myself also to be present at it, in a sense, simply by virtue of being a China sailor. The time came when I retold those yarns to men still younger than myself. For me, and I think for many of us, those stories had become generalized into part of the romantic aura which overhung duty on the China Station.

From my present vantage point I can understand, as I could not when I was a functioning part of it, that the sailor folk-mind was transforming that episode of Chinese history into a myth. It was all being done by oral expression and oral transmission. The men who were doing it were not consciously motivated in what they were doing nor even consciously aware of it. It was a folk-mind at work, abstracting certain incidents which seemed to it expressive and exemplary of the times and making them into a cycle of folk-tales.

The living myth, for such it was, died when the members of the subculture which made and nourished it were either killed or dispersed. That happened when World War II erupted into the old China Station and destroyed the old U. S. Asiatic Fleet as irrevocably as Humpty Dumpty.

Let me now briefly recount that myth, the matrix in which the folk-tales were embedded. Please bear in mind that I am not, repeat *not*, recounting history. Very well, then.

In 1925, "troubles," or antiforeign activity, sharply increased in China. In 1926 the lid blew off. The storm center was a new warlord named Chiang Kai-shek, and he was bowling over all the other warlords like duckpins. He had Russian advisers, and he meant to chase all the palefaces out of China. His troops took over and used mission properties on a scale never before dared by other warlords. In the river ports he controlled, foreigners, including sailors on shore leave, were subjected to unheard-of in-

dignities. The gunboats were fired upon from ambush more frequently and more severely than ever before.

From Washington came orders that the gunboats were not to deal with this increased trouble in the traditional ways. Patrols ashore were not to let themselves be provoked into using violence. Ships fired upon from ambush were not to return the fire unless its source could be clearly seen and pinpointed. In practice, it nearly always could not be. Gunboat captains varied as to what they considered sufficient clarity, and morale aboard their ships varied accordingly. But the general morale level steadily declined.

The sailors were the victims of a split in the American community in China. Many businessmen contended, and the sailors agreed with them, that the new warlord and his people could be made to behave properly by some judicious Naval gunfire at the right time and place. Forbearance, they insisted, only invited more encroachment. The missionaries proclaimed that the new warlord was really the Chinese George Washington and warned that fighting him would start a major war. They wanted all the gunboats taken out of China. The upshot was that the gunboats had to stay, but they were not allowed to fight.

The missionaries were taking the worst beating of any foreign group in China, and still they backed Chiang. They thought that if they helped him get rid of the gunboats and businessmen he would, in reward, permit them to keep their own very good deal in China. The missionary version of conditions in China was the one believed in America because they could spread it at the grassroots among the millions of ordinary people who contributed to missions. And those grassroots people controlled Congress and the President.

Please remember that I am only outlining a myth.

The British were also having missionary trouble. A grotesque situation developed in which the gunboats of the five major treaty powers were competing in meekness. The British meekly

let an unarmed mob take their concession at Hankow away from them, and not long afterward London meekly signed away British rights to it. The myth put great significance on that first fleck of mortar falling away from the imperial foundations. The Japanese had no Christian missionaries to tie their hands, yet they were being meekest of all. For years the Japanese had been singled out for a trade boycott in China, and they were happy to see Chinese hostility being displayed toward the British and Americans. The Japanese were operating on the theory that the meekest were going to inherit the trade of China.

Now I must interrupt the myth for an interpretation of which I am not at all sure. I have seen men, when they were telling of missionary behavior at that time, redden and clench their fists. I have heard their voices grow thick with anger. When American missionaries meekly permitted themselves to be robbed and slapped and cursed, they were making America lose face. But when, by their machinations in Washington, they forced men in U.S. Naval uniform meekly to endure being stoned and cursed and spat upon, when they forced United States warships in full commission to flee out of range of hostile fire without returning it, they were perhaps doing something worse than simply tarnishing the national honor. They may have been verging upon treason. They seemed to be aiding the forces of evil while pretending, as always, to be the sole custodians of the good. I think it must have been some such unarticulated feeling in the sailor folk-mind which steel-edged the mythic rage directed against the missionaries. And now let me continue the myth.

The missionaries were not having it all their own way. After the loss of Hankow, the British ordered more land and sea forces to the Far East. So did France. Spain, Holland, and Portugal sent warships to Shanghai. The U.S. Navy started three more cruisers for China, and the missionaries short-stopped them in Pearl Harbor. The Fourth Marine Regiment got as far as Shanghai, but

the missionaries kept it from coming ashore. The men had to wait for weeks packed like sardines in their transport on the Whangpoo River. Chiang's army came steadily down the Yangtze Valley toward Shanghai. The last large intervening city held by the old warlord was Nanking. In Shanghai an uprising wrested control of the native city from that warlord, and the foreign concessions were ringed by hostile mobs.

Meanwhile, in Nanking, still blaming their troubles on the presence of the gunboats, some hundred American missionaries were signing and publishing still another petition asking President Coolidge to withdraw the gunboats from China. A few weeks later Chiang's troops took Nanking. They began very brutal treatment of the foreigners, including rape and murder. The American consul, trapped in the city, signaled the American warships in the river to lay down a curtain of shellfire around the place where he had taken refuge. Such had become the grotesque state of things in China that the American destroyer captains almost dared not obey. As myth so often does from crucial moments of history, this myth abstracts from that moment a suitably expressive utterance.

"Well, here I go for a medal or a court-martial," stoutly said Captain Roy Smith of the U.S.S. *Noa*. "Commence firing!"

The American guns roared. After an interval just long enough to make it clear who had fired first, the British cruiser *Emerald* joined in. Presumably her captain murmured something about blood being thicker than water. That is another mythic utterance deriving from an earlier Anglo-Saxon battle with the Chinese. Meek to the last, the Japanese gunboats at Nanking did not fire at all.

A few salvoes settled everything. The consul escaped. The American admiral rushed to the scene and gave the Chinese general an ultimatum: deliver the foreigners without further harm and without delay or the allied squadron would level the city. The Chinese general saw the light and meekly delivered them.

Down in Shanghai the Fourth Marines finally went ashore.

The Sixth Marines in San Diego and the Thirty-first Infantry in Manila began embarking for China. The three stalled cruisers left Pearl Harbor on a speed-run for China. Chiang Kai-shek saw the light.

He dismissed the Russians and got rid of the troublemakers in his forces. Very quickly the trouble along the Yangtze dropped to the customary nuisance level. Both gunboats and missionaries were soon back in business as usual. Even the Japanese Navy saved face in the end. One of the Japanese Naval officers from Nanking went down to Shanghai, made a formal report to his admiral, and then formally did hara-kiri upon himself. He became the martyred hero of the myth.

Finally, and most edifying of all, the missionaries saw the light. Their leaders, including many who had signed the Nanking Petition, published another signed statement. In it they admitted their error, accepted their guilt for the suffering it had caused, and hoped that God would forgive them.

That concludes the myth. All of these events really happened, and yet it is important to remember that I have here been recounting not history but a myth.

Many years after I had learned and helped to propagate that myth, years during which I had almost forgotten it, I tried to write one of its constituent yarns into a short story. I had great trouble with it.

I found I could not bring out the story values until I had explained why Chinese soldiers were dangerous, why there should be such strong antipathy between sailors and missionaries, and what the gunboats were doing in China in the first place. I finally wrote a rather long story in which the train of events did not quite reach the story I had meant to tell. I had only set the stage for that story.

My agent, Rogers Terrill, a very wise and perceptive man in matters literary, saw then that I had hold of a novel. He urged me to write it. I disagreed and tried again to write the short story. I

fell short of it again in the same way, and then I was convinced. I could not tell that story out of context, and I could not develop the context except at novel length.

It would have been simple to use the myth-context in which I knew the story. But I thought few people any longer believed that old myth. I did not think I believed it myself, although my sailor-protagonist would have to believe it. But in the interval I had become an educated man, and I knew that myth was not history and, in order to be the omniscient author, I felt I had to learn the actual history.

I read some hundreds of books and all I could find of the contemporary periodicals treating of events in China during those years. I learned about the unequal treaties which so gravely impaired Chinese sovereignty. Chiang Kai-shek wanted to unify China and restore her lost sovereignty. The palefaces were not necessarily to be driven into the sea; they would be free to stay on in China, but only with Chinese consent and subject to Chinese law, as in any other sovereign nation. The gunboats would have to go, of course. On that one point the myth was accurate.

By no means all the missionaries wished to see China granted full sovereignty. The minority of Americans in China who did wish it were not all missionaries. The turn-the-other-cheek orders enforced on the gunboats seemed hardly due at all to missionary machinations in Washington. It seemed more the embarrassment of a nation genuinely devoted to human liberty and trembling on a critical point of being no longer able to rationalize the incongruous position it held in China. Another factor was postwar isolationist sentiment. Unlike most Americans in China, Americans at home were reluctant to believe that the *status quo* in China was even just, much less worth a war to preserve it.

In those days something pretty important was hanging in the balance in China. On that both myth and history agreed.

In my research I was pleased to discover one by one the actual incidents which underlay the yarns I knew. I was interested to

note the considerable changes many of them had undergone in becoming folk-tales. But for a long time one of the most important yarns, which I wanted to make into a key episode in my novel, eluded me. That was the martyrdom of the coolie Po-han.

I finally found it in the *Hankow Herald*, the English-language newspaper published nearest to the scene of action in *Sand Pebbles*. Even there, Po-han's death received only three lines of passing mention in a long news story about troubles upriver. I wondered how the contemporary press could have almost completely ignored it when the myth gave it such prominence. I wondered whether I should not eliminate it from the novel. Then I found it a second time, in the 1926 *Survey of International Affairs*. From all the confused welter of events in China of that year, Arnold Toynbee had also found Po-han's small death worthy of inclusion in the record.

When I thought I had in mind the truth of history as exactly as I could determine it, I began trying to make it into a novel. Once again I met trouble.

There was far too much history. I would have to select only sample bits of it. I drafted a plot-structure of four interwoven and parallel story lines: one each for a gunboat, a mission, a foreign business firm, and a Chinese family. It seemed impossible to accommodate the history in any smaller compass. Very soon I found my reach had exceeded my grasp several times over. It was far too much for a single book. I could only persuade myself to take out the last three stories by promising myself that I would write them later as separate but related novels, after the fashion of *The Alexandria Quartet*. Even then, narrowed down to the gunboat story, I had trouble.

Technical considerations, such as viewpoint limitation, and more literary considerations, such as the classical unities, made it difficult for me to include much of the history that I wanted to use. I found myself insensibly shifting real events in space and

time and modifying them in other ways. I saw that I was warping my plot-structure in some ways and warping history in other ways in an effort to make the two coincide. And where they were going to coincide, I began to see, was in the very myth pattern I had set out to avoid.

That realization became one of the crises of my writing career. Somberly I thought my way back through the history. It began to seem to me that, even while it was happening, it was myth. I mean that was the only way the history could get into the newspapers and into people's minds. The sailor-myth, in more sophisticated form, functioned for conservative opinion. A counter-myth, carried principally by the social gospel missionaries, served for the liberal minority. Beyond them I seemed to discern also a Chinese myth and counter-myth.

Then those times seemed to me one of clashing myths, each voracious to devour and to assimilate the history as fast as it happened, each eliminating to oblivion all that was unsuitable to its metabolism. Each myth was trying to eat all the other myths. I began to think and I still think that, wherever there is selection and emphasis by human agency, there will be myth. I doubted that even historians could write history. And I knew I had no choice myself except to write a myth.

Knowing that, I decided to make my myth as many-sided and inclusive as I could. I put a subsidiary viewpoint into a missionary and brought back in some of the mission story, the better to interweave the liberal counter-myth. Through my Chinese characters I tried to weave in minor strands of the clashing Chinese myths. I was most resolute not to judge of right or wrong among them. I meant to give them a fair field and no favor. After that, the writing went very well for me until I neared the end. Then I fumbled badly.

I tried to make the missionary myth triumph and survive at one remote, imaginary place in China. I made the words obey my

personal will, and I wrote the ending that way. Both my agent and my editor, M. S. Wyeth at Harper's, took strong exception to it. They said it rang false as a tin dollar. They did not try to tell me what the ending should be. They simply insisted that I had not yet found it.

By degrees, grudgingly, against my own strong resistance, I did find it. Without the help of my agent and editor I could not have done so. We were all three by then bound into a kind of rapport with the novel which I think is unusual in writing and editing. As a matter of fact, the key insight, that Jake Holman had to die, came to Rogers Terrill in a dream. He awoke and called me long distance to tell me about it. At once all the pieces fell into place for me, and I could see the ending in all of its inescapable truth. I wrote with power and certainty again and finished the novel successfully.

The experience taught me that, while myth is not literally true, it has a kind of truth proper to itself and the power to insist upon it. I could not enforce my personal will upon the myth which finally ate the history. Because of the ending of *Sand Pebbles*, one reviewer has called me "remorseless as Sophocles." Flattering as I find the comparison, I must disavow it. I wrote that ending with pity and reluctance. It was the myth that was remorseless.

In concluding, I must remember that I promised not to draw any general conclusions. Writing *Sand Pebbles* was a long, deep-running, very private and personal experience, and what I learned from it is not necessarily valid for anyone other than myself. With that qualification, here is what I think I have learned about the relation of history to historical fiction.

History is an ideal which the best of men can only hope to approximate. Wherever there is selection and emphasis by human agency, there will be myth. No man can live a day of his normal life, much less write a book, without selecting narrowly

from all that competes for his attention. What governs his selections and the emphasis he places upon them will be his myth. There is no evading it, in book or life. The most one can do is to enlarge his myth, to make room within it for as many of its rival myths as he can, and to grant to all of them all that he can of their own peculiar truth and justice.

From a speech at the New York Herald Tribune *and A.B.A. Luncheon, New York, N.Y., February 18, 1963*

Our Own Houses

∾ ALTHOUGH I knew very well the importance of book reviews, it was the verdicts of the people who were actually in Central China in 1926 that I awaited with greatest anxiety after the publication of *Sand Pebbles*. I have now heard from a good many of these people, and I am happy to report that they all say *Sand Pebbles* vividly recreates those times in Central China just as they remember them. I am at least as proud of that as I am of any other distinction the book has won.

Most of the letters, understandably, are from old gunboat sailors. A man in Philadelphia was chief engineer of one of those old ex-Spanish gunboats when she went aground for three days far up the Yangtze River. When they got her off, she had a thump in her engine which he tried for a year to take out and could not. That was in 1916. He wrote me utterly convinced that I had gone aboard his old ship ten years later and taken out the knock and finally written the experience into a story. He thought the repair job a more praiseworthy feat than the novel. Reluctantly, I had to tell him I thought I had invented that faulty engine and could take no credit for repairing it except on paper.

It was not too hard for me to recreate those times from a Naval viewpoint because I was myself a young sailor in China just a few years after the revolution. I had only to extrapolate the attitudes and behavior of the men I knew a few years backward into a scene which had not changed much physically. But when I tried in my imagination to experience that history as a Chinese, and as an American civilian in China, it was more difficult. I did much research into contemporary sources. I studied hundreds of

letters to the editor in newspapers and magazines, trying my hardest to be the writer and to think and feel and say those words myself. In a strange way, I made myself become a Chinese and a missionary as well as a sailor, all in the same body. It was a weirdly illuminating experience, of which I shall say more in a moment. When I finished the writing, I had some small doubts about the Naval consensus, but I was most anxious about the others.

I have not heard from any Chinese yet, but letters from a number of businessmen and missionaries have arrived to reassure me. A recent one is from a married couple who were on the staff of a mission school in Wuchang, across the river from Hankow, during the period of *Sand Pebbles*. They write: "It seems amazing to us that you have been able in your novel to be so very accurate in your details and to show so fairly and correctly the attitudes of the many conflicting groups."

I always knew that to be my most formidable writing problem. I had to depict a three-way conflict. The feeling was bitter and passionate. While I was living my way back into it I was reminded strongly of the conflict then raging in Algeria. In time I found myself taking all three sides with equal clarity and emotional conviction.

Now I know that any psychologist will insist that no sane man can do such a thing. It was not something I did, however; it simply happened to me. Perhaps I was technically mad, but I felt quite natural. It was not until the writing was finished and I began coming back to my own proper and contemporary person that I experienced briefly the full strangeness of it. Today it is hardly more than a memory. Some of the effects, however, I think are permanent. I went into the experience strongly on the Navy side, although not blindly partisan, and I came out of it much nearer to the side of the liberal missionaries. Now I am having trouble believing in the reality of my own past self.

Let me summarize that three-way conflict in China. Seven European nations, the United States, and Japan had treaties with

China which in certain ways gravely impaired Chinese sovereignty. The Chinese wanted to get rid of the unequal treaties, as they called them. In effect, they were demanding immediate and unconditional independence. The liberal missionaries favored granting their demand. That is only the bare bones of it; I have not the time to state it more fully.

What shook me, what still shakes me, is that I could have spent nearly ten years in China after that revolution was crushed without becoming more than vaguely aware that the unequal treaties existed. I never knew they were so bitterly offensive to so many Chinese. Yet I was not stupid. I had a fair education. I talked to many people ashore, and I read the newspapers. I cannot explain to myself why I did not know.

I have tried very hard to recall what I and my shipmates on half a dozen different ships in China knew and thought and said about the unequal treaties. We knew that we were protecting Americans in China. We knew that we were not subject to Chinese law, but only to the U.S. Court for China. We knew that it was all right to curse and kick coolies in China, but that you had better not do anything like that in Japan or the Philippines. We knew that our ships could go anywhere they pleased in China without the diplomatic arrangements necessary for any visit to Japan. That was all part of the lore passed along to newcomers on the China Station.

It was never passed along to me that all of it was by virtue of a treaty between the United States and China. We seemed simply to take it for granted, like the climate and geography of China. It was just the way things were, had been, and would always be, and no sailor in my hearing ever questioned it.

We never questioned foreign control of the Chinese Customs, although some of us hoped to get jobs in the Customs Service when we retired in China. We did not know that the treaties permitted China to levy only a flat 5 per cent tariff on all imports, a rate unchanged since the master-treaty was imposed on China in 1842. We did not know that a great part of the Customs reve-

nue went as interest payments to foreign bondholders without so much as passing through Chinese hands. The principal way in which all that impinged upon our lives was by making whisky very cheap in China.

A quart of good Scotch whisky over the counter at Gande Price or Caldbeck McGregor in Shanghai cost a dollar and fifteen cents. At the Fourth Marines Regimental Club on Bubbling Well Road we could buy it duty-free at a dollar and five cents. The U.S. Naval Purchasing Office in Shanghai would authenticate chits for us permitting us to buy duty-free whisky by the case. Chief petty officers could have one case a week. Lesser petty officers such as myself could only have one case a month. What most of us did was to sign our allowances over to bartenders, who thereby bought their bar stock duty-free. Most of them kept a pad of the forms back of the bar, just for that purpose.

When I finally returned to the States in 1941, I came ashore in San Francisco with one of my Shanghai shipmates, and we walked up Market Street. We were looking all around. The shops were no more impressive than the ones along Nanking Road, we told each other. Then we came to a drugstore with a great streamer sign advertising a cut-rate liquor sale. In the window, the prize bargain of the day was an array of pint bottles of our favorite Scotch whisky. The price on each was two dollars and twenty-nine cents.

"*Pints!*" we both said, unbelievingly.

We looked at each other with a wild surmise. Craig spoke first.

"I guess we're back in the land of the free, all right," he said ruefully.

Well, those were good old days and they are gone forever and I am glad they are gone. I find more discomfort than pleasure now in those memories. They make me wonder what I may be taking casually for granted right this moment which could seem equally incredible to me thirty years from now, if it is granted me to live that much longer.

From a speech before the North Carolina Literary Forum, Raleigh, N. C., March 28, 1963

The Writer's Materials

❧ THAT a group of writers find it quite natural to talk in turn on an identical subject is indicative of something about our craft which I fear is imperfectly understood by many who aspire to enter it. That is the uniquely individual set of writing habits each of us must find for himself by trial and error. There is hardly any such thing as "the writer," taken generically. There are only individual persons who write in ways that vary endlessly. There are as many different talks about any aspect of writing as there are writers to make them.

I want to preface my remarks with a warning. We gain something valuable by studying the work-habits of other writers, but it is never a formula which we can use for ourselves. It is more nearly an assurance that no such general formula exists. In my early days, every attempt I made to take over directly some work-habit of another writer turned out in the end to be harmful. We write best when we are wholly ourselves. I hope no one will ever try to take over one of my work-habits for no better reason than that it happens to work for me.

When I ask myself what my materials are, it seems to me that I cannot exclude anything. I use the whole of my life. I use all that I have experienced and observed and been told of and thought about in solitude and read about in books. A very great deal of it has come from books. I am convinced that all of it, however acquired, enters in some subtle way into everything I write. It is a poetic fancy that when a little girl plucks a flower the courses of distant worlds are altered. In Newtonian gravitational theory that is a consequence of any displacement of mass, how-

ever slight. It does not matter if the effect be too slight to be measured; it is just pleasant to believe in it. It is an affirmation of a very primitive philosophical notion, the sympathy of the whole, which it still pleases me to believe true. That is how I think it is with my writing. I believe in man as microcosm and in all sorts of outmoded poetic notions, because I am sure they help me to write.

It is not wholly a matter of faith. Any time I wish to look for it, I can find evidence. Once when I was very young and distressed, my grandmother gave me a piece of pink candy flavored with wintergreen. Now, when I write of pain and distress, there is often a faint odor of wintergreen about it, and sometimes it will get into the story. That would have made good sense to Coleridge, who knew all about associations. Now that we can speak of Pavlovian conditioning and stimulus generalization and demonstrate it all in rats, we are less ready to admit it in ourselves. Perhaps we feel that we are thereby diminished and made rat-like. I prefer to feel that the rats are thereby made more wonderful than I had once thought them to be. It is those endlessly linked associations of which I have been speaking that tie together the lives of rats and men and lead me to believe that when I am writing with all my power I have the resources of the whole of my life just behind the tip of my pencil.

It should be simpler, then, to talk about how I select from all my material that which finally goes down in words on paper to comprise a particular story. It should be simpler, but it is not. I have to pretend to myself that I am making a conscious, rational choice of material, but I think my writing prospers in direct proportion to my failure in actually doing so. How it works is best illustrated by a few examples.

In the spring of 1958 I made a conscious decision to write my first straight-fiction short story. My conscious choice for the germ of it was a yarn I had heard told by sailors in a bar in Shanghai thirty years ago. One factor in the yarn was an unnamed mission

station. My first bit of writing work was to select a name for the mission. I began it while riding with Manly Wellman down to a vacation in New Orleans. He and I discussed dozens of possible names, none of which pleased me. In the process we talked about missions. Manly was born and grew into his fundamental world-awareness in a mission station at the edge of the unknown in Darkest Africa. Certain nuances of his childhood experience came over to me and later colored my story, but I did not fix upon a name.

Weeks later, when I was thinking of something else, the name "China Light" popped unbidden into my awareness. I knew at once that it was perfect.

I had also to select a name for my fictional gunboat. I went about it very methodically. The historical gunboat that wintered at Changsha was named *Villalobos*. Her nickname was "The Village Hobo," and her crew called themselves Village Hoboes, Changsha being the village. I set out to select a fictional Spanish name from which I could derive an analogous nickname. It happened that the old ex-Spanish gunboat I knew best was named *San Felipe*, so I began trying saint's names. I tried a lot of them, including *San Pablo*, and none pleased me. It was something I turned to at odd moments over a period of weeks. One day the nickname "Sand Pebble" split off from *San Pablo*, and it pleased me very much. The river at Changsha is wide and shallow and full of long sandbars. Changsha itself means "long sand" in Chinese. A ship stranded there for the winter by low water was said by Yangtze River sailors to be "sitting on a sandbar." That would seem to explain adequately how and why I chose that particular name.

There is much more to it, however. Since earliest childhood I have been fond of rocks. As a boy I collected them. From the moment I began trying to write professionally I have kept several pebbles on my desk. They are as much guardian spirits as paperweights. In Chapel Hill I live on the bank of a steep ravine, and I have laboriously carried up from the creek scores of water-

worn stones to make borders for flower beds. The flowers bloom brightly and pass, but the stones are always there. Very many times I have stood on the banks of a stream and held a pebble of quartzite or feldspar in my hand and simply thought about it.

Once it was an unbounded little region of a great sleeping bed of stone deep under the earth. For millions of years it lay there undergoing slow metamorphoses by heat and pressure and chemical change. Then for more millions of years it was folded and twisted and uplifted and carved by running water into mountains. It was laid bare at long last to the light of day. Frost and the living roots of plants wedged free a fragment. The stream tumbled it against other fragments, moving it a stage downstream with each flood, letting it rest in the intervals, but always polishing and shaping it. The stream has given it a unique form and texture and has made it exist as a separated thing in the world.

So it has come to my hand, and no human eyes have ever really looked at it before. It is an *encounter* for both of us. Here I meet it in mid-journey of a particulate existence that may have begun before Christ was born and may not finish until after Christ comes again. Where it will finish is in a loss of identity by diffusion of its particles through a bed of sediments, which will in time become stone and go once more through the cycle. But this particular pebble will not be a second time. He and I are brothers.

I had none of these thoughts present in my conscious mind when I chose the nickname of my fictional gunboat. I am convinced, however, that they were part of the choosing agency at work somewhere beyond the myopic range of my conscious attention. If I had chosen a different nickname, I would have written a different book.

For I did write a book, and not the short story I had chosen to write. My literary agent recognized it as a novel long before I was willing to concede that I could not make it a short story. A

large part of my learning to write has been learning how to recognize those signals from the unconscious and how to give way to them gracefully while still maintaining discipline.

As soon as I began work on the China story I developed a great thirst to read about China. I spent many days in the stacks of the UNC library reading files of newspapers and magazines. I went up to the New York Public Library to read files of newspapers not available at Chapel Hill. In New York I searched the second-hand bookstores and bought more than a hundred books on China. I read other hundreds of books on China borrowed from many libraries. They were books of history, geography, commerce, travel, description, diplomatic dispatches, literary and philosophical essays, and personal memoirs of all sorts and conditions of people. They covered every part of China and ranged in time from the middle of the last century up to the present.

I had little notion of what precisely I was looking for. I seemed simply to need to take into myself off the printed page all I could obtain of the whole of China. As I read, I began to recognize a signal, a now-and-then quickening of an already lively interest. It indicated something that I was going to use in the novel. Certain places in the novel would become clear to me for the first time at such moments. I always included such material in the sketchy notes I made. Later, sometimes several years later, when I came to use it, I would check my notes or even go back to the source in order to have it more fully. Each time I would find that I already had it in my head as fully as I was going to use it.

Another area of my material was my memory of all my own years in China. I explored and reviewed them. I would put myself to sleep at night by re-experiencing in memory all that I could recover of my time in China. I would walk down a particular street or along some riverfront or lean on the rail of my gunboat and watch some particular stretch of landscape move slowly by. As time passed, the colors became more vivid and the outlines sharper. The scenes took on more detail. Sound and scent came faintly in. Sometimes I would recognize in my visual memo-

THE WRITER'S MATERIALS/123

ries something I knew I had not seen myself but had only read about. What I was reading and what I was remembering were beginning to mingle and fuse together at some unconscious level.

While I was doing all that, I was also trying to write, first the short story and then the novel. I had to start over repeatedly, and I threw away hundreds of painfully-wrought pages. I worked at it for more than two years before a certain bold assurance came into the feeling as I wrote and I knew that I really had hold of my novel. That was roughly about the time when I began to notice the mingling and fusing of what I was reading with what I was remembering. I think that period of intensive unconscious preparation was necessary before I could begin writing with real assurance.

What went on during that time? It is impossible to know. My own belief is that the material was assembled and the selections made from it and formed into the story at a level below my awareness. It may have been essential to the process that I be consciously all the while trying and failing to write the story. I would like to think that all the work I threw away was not really wasted. When I *really* began writing the story, however, my problem was to hold my personal judgments and desires enough in abeyance to let the story take shape in words on paper without crippling distortion. Where there are flaws in the finished work, and there are flaws, it is where I failed in that.

There would have been many more flaws if I had not had the help of a very skilled and understanding editor. Different writers may need different sorts of help from their editors, but I wonder if it may not all reduce in the end to the editor enabling an already-formed story to take its own proper shape in words on paper despite the manifold obstructions the writer himself cannot help putting in the way.

What I have said to this point, in substance, is that my material is everything I know, and probably much that I do not know consciously, and that all new knowledge I take into myself must

become somehow assimilated to my lived experience before I can make effective use of it in putting words on paper. But there is another kind of material without which I could not write, and I want to mention it briefly before concluding these remarks.

I hardly know what to call it: life-energy, perhaps, or something like that; I can best define it by telling how I use it. I have to withdraw it progressively from the contemporary world around me. It all goes somehow into the work that I am doing. I stop reading the newspapers. I become increasingly reluctant to answer the telephone. I begin refusing to go out in the evening except on weekends. Then I begin to grudge the weekends. When I am doing my very best writing, I almost cease to exist as a person. I will go days at a time hardly speaking at all, even to my wife. I think I am then in what psychologists would call a light trance state. Whatever tends to force me out of it I find annoying and painful and a threat to the work I am doing. I believe the greatest single advantage I had in writing *Sand Pebbles* was a set of life-circumstances which enabled me to make and sustain that creative withdrawal.

When I finished *Sand Pebbles* it was like coming out of solitary confinement. I felt a sense of loss and all sorts of strange distresses. I could not at once re-engage myself with the passing flow of life. Then I was caught up in it until I have sometimes lately felt like a chip of wood in a millrace. It has more often than not been very pleasant and exciting, but for nearly a year now I have not written anything of large scope.

I have another story planned, and this time I know it is a novel. I have done a lot of thinking about it when I could find the time, and I have begun reading the books. Frequently at night I review memories. I hope that during this year of seeming idleness the process of unconscious preparation has been going steadily forward, so that when I begin my compulsive, necessary withdrawal in another month or so the writing I do will not have to be thrown wholly away. I am going to try very hard to reconstitute the circumstances under which I wrote *Sand Pebbles*.

From a speech before the University Woman's Club, Chapel Hill, N. C., April 18, 1963

Journey with a Little Man

〜 IF I have learned anything in the process of becoming a professional writer, it is that there are as many ways of becoming a writer as there are writers. I am going to talk only about the way that worked for me. The thought of becoming a writer first came to me as an occasional idle fancy during World War II. It did not become a firm decision until about 1950. Then I planned it rather carefully. I planned first to get a formal education and then to serve my writing apprenticeship in science fiction. That field pays poorly, so I thought I would not meet much skilled competition. It would also allow me to indulge the very great interest I had in all areas of science. My plan became my excuse for taking far more science courses than my major in English literature would conventionally accommodate.

Often on my way through school I was tempted to give up my plan. I read everything and listened to everything with a perpetual "What if?" before me. Many answers which suggested themselves fascinated me. By each science in turn I was tempted to forego writing and take to asking "What if?" directly of nature. It seemed to me then and does still that science is as much a creative activity as art. Both are concerned with discovery and fabrication. Science is the art of the intellect.

What held me back each time was the conviction that only as a writer would I remain free to range across the whole of human experience and to mix intellect with feeling. I wanted to present new and fascinating ideas from science in the form of stories. I always assumed that when the time came to write the stories I

would find it as simple a matter as writing term papers. Seldom have I been more wrong.

I had one experience in a science course which, if I had understood it fully, might have spared me much anguish when I began writing. It was an experiment in a psychology lab which took me through what I now consider to be a learning process of the same kind as learning creative writing. It is worth recounting in some detail.

That morning in class the instructor had told us that between any conscious intention and the completed act lies an apparatus of nerves and primitive brain centers not under control of the conscious mind. I understood and accepted the statement.

The lab was in the afternoon. It was a fine summer day, and several of the girls came to the lab barefoot. The lab instructor formed us into teams of two, and one of the barefoot girls fell to me as partner. She was to be the experimenter and I the subject. My task was to trace a pencil over a large five-pointed star printed on a sheet of paper while I saw my hand and the star only in a mirror. The girl would time me and record how often and how widely my pencil strayed from the printed line.

I always tried to do well in that psych lab. I think I wanted to prove that my reflexes had not slowed down. That day in particular I wanted to do well. While we waited for the signal to begin, I thought out carefully the principles of mirror-reversal. I was going to use my knowledge of optics and geometry to give me an advantage over the other subjects. The girl smiled what I took to be encouragement at me. We were facing each other across a table, and all around the large room other couples were similarly awaiting the signal.

"Go!" the instructor said.

The girl clicked her stopwatch. My pencil went wildly off. I paused and thought quickly again through the geometry. When I knew exactly how my hand should move, I so moved it. Again it went skating awry with a will all its own. That happened again and again as I tried to reason my way through and to make my

hand obey me. I felt a most peculiar, dismayed frustration at the disobedience of my hand. It began to seem like an entity separate from myself. It would rush clear off the paper. If only the girl had not been there, I could have cursed it. All around me the other subjects were finishing their first trial. I knew I was sweating and red-faced. The girl was plainly sorry for me, and that made it worse. I was her team and I was failing her.

Finally, in despair, I simply went at it by trial and error. That was not much better. I seesawed painfully along. When I had to change direction, my whole arm would freeze. I would will it to move and it would not. I could start the pencil tracing again only by moving my whole body from the waist. I was the last one in the class to finish the first trial, and my trace was eleven times longer than the line I was trying to follow. I was ashamed to look at the girl.

I did better on succeeding trials. I found I could set up a random tremor in the pencil point and somehow simply *wish* it along in the right direction. I began feeling better, and on each trial the tremor became less pronounced. At the end of the period the girl gave me a difficult pattern to trace, a complex affair of straight and curved lines. I yawed wildly off when I began it, but I did not call upon any optics or geometry. I just steadied on the course and wished my way on around it, and my score on it was one of the best in the class.

When I wrote up the experiment I said it demonstrated that the neural complex below the level of conscious awareness can be trained to a new mode of action only by trial and error. If a general principle is involved, the complex will, with enough trials, learn that also and be able to apply it in a new situation. The conscious mind may already know the principle perfectly and still be unable to apply it until it is also learned, slowly and painfully, by the unconscious part.

I should have written "unconscious partner." I should have pondered the implications of that experience more deeply than I did.

When I finished school I married, with a clear understanding between my wife and me that I was going to become a writer, and I settled in to write. My attitude was very matter-of-fact. I was going to set words end to end as methodically as masons lay bricks end to end. I studied books and articles about writing and abstracted from them all a list of rules by which to write. Then I sat down at the dining-room table to apply what I knew.

I found I could not. The words simply would not come. With all those rules in my mind I was like the fabled centipede who could not run for worrying which leg came after which. What little I wrote had about as much life in it as a brick wall. I scorned it myself. However, when I laid aside the rules, the writing went the opposite way. What was planned to be a neat 5,000 words would explode to 30,000 and leave me feeling like the sorcerer's apprentice.

The writing I did the second way pleased me too much. When I would try to apply the rules in rewriting, I felt distinctly that I was maiming living literature in favor of dead rule books. I applied them rather too gently, as I know now. I would send beautiful manuscripts fluttering off to the marketplace. They would come creeping back to me out of the dust and heat with printed rejection slips clamped in their ugly beaks.

That went on for more than a year. I became increasingly grim. I refused to believe that I could not write. I felt intolerably exasperated at my powerlessness to do as I willed. My plan had gone wrong, somehow. Originally I had meant to live in the Nevada desert, alone except for books, and to write there. I will not expand on the painful months during which the conviction grew in me that I would have to go to the desert. At last I could bear it no longer, and I proposed to my wife a trial separation both from her and from Chapel Hill.

I stood at that moment in the greatest danger of my life. I know now that no writer can have a better wife than I have nor a better place in which to write than Chapel Hill, where I found her. What I really had to have is what I have since come to call "crea-

tive isolation." I would have found that in the desert and misinterpreted it. But I will always be grateful that I gained it in a much less drastic way.

I took an office downtown. It had no telephone. Neither my wife nor anyone else was ever to come there and disturb me. Every morning before eight o'clock I would lock myself in with a thermos of coffee and a sandwich. I would not come out again until after five o'clock. I did that seven days a week.

From the first day, much of my anguish left me. I recognized it as the same I had felt in the psychology lab. My confidence and drive came back. I could read stories that were the best I could do six months before and see flaws all through them. I realized that all the while I had thought I was stopped cold I had really been making progress. I was midway in just such a process of unconscious learning as tracing that star had been.

Learning to write creatively is a process of training the unconscious, I decided. We all have an unconscious personality component, a silent partner in all we think we do alone. In some learning situations that silent partner can lag far behind his conscious partner. Mirror drawing is one such situation, and learning to write creatively is another.

That insight into my work saved me from a disastrous mistake in the other part of my life. It remained to act upon it in a way which would forward my work. Isolation was a necessary but not a sufficient condition. Fortunately, the others were easier to discover.

The first step was to attain and hold what I came to call "the writing mood." I had never experienced it before I began working in that office. It was a kind of inner excitement, a bit like waiting for a curtain to rise upon something unknown and wonderful. I learned to evoke it in various ways: wandering idly about the office and trying not to think at all; sitting at my desk toying with my pencil and a blank sheet of paper; reading poetry aloud to myself. At first it always took me several hours to evoke it, and distressingly often I could not evoke it all day long.

I learned not to fret about that. The one certain way not to attain the mood was to grasp for it with grim resolution. I had to *not-care* before it would come. Once attained, it was most precarious. A knock on my door and the necessity to speak even a few words would banish it for hours. A trip to the barbershop would destroy a whole day for me. Sometimes I became quite shaggy while I strove to finish a short story, and I could almost envy a bald man.

I wrote only when I was in the mood. Certain strange aspects of it came to my attention. I would write half a page and realize with a start that an hour or more had passed in what seemed like a few minutes. An observer would no doubt have seen me sitting frozen for minutes at a time, but I never had the sense of it. Often I would be up and away from my desk before I realized that I was pacing. At first, with the lingering conviction that one would never get a brick wall built that way, I would sit resolutely down again. That always broke the mood. But if I simply went on pacing I would before long find myself back at my desk and writing with no memory of having first willed it.

On days when I could not reach the mood I would do research for my stories. I read through many a science textbook, making notes and stopping to reflect and feeling the same pleasant excitement as when I was in school. That was a different excitement, more of an intellectual excitement. The writing mood was visceral; I could feel it vaguely across my midriff. Sometimes I would try to study Maugham or Kipling or some other master of the short story to learn technique. I could not deal with them as with the textbooks. After a paragraph or two I would be swept away by the story and only catch myself shirking duty after several pages. The trouble, and the familiar frustration, I knew how to explain to myself.

By then, strictly for my own purposes, I had postulated an unconscious part of myself which I personified and named "the little man in the subbasement." It was a game, and I played it as

children do, only half-believing and half aware in delightful balance that it was only make-believe. I was not being scientific; I was simply trying very hard to learn to write. I never thought then that someday I would talk about it publicly. I find now, however, that I cannot tell how I became a professional writer without giving the little man his share of blame and credit. *He* was the one who was shirking duty when we read Maugham together.

Whatever I wrote when I was "in the mood" was better than I had done before. I began getting a few scrawled words and initials on the printed rejection slips. Then I began getting handwritten notes of rejection. Six months after I began work in my office, just as the Christmas holidays of 1957 set in, I received a formal letter of rejection. It pushed me across what I now consider to be the barrier between amateur and professional writing.

The rejected manuscript ran to 14,000 words. The editor told me that I had story enough for only 7,000 words. If I could compress it to that, he would be willing to read it again. It was not a promise of a sale. But it was the first expression of interest I had gotten in almost two years of steady work, and it energized me powerfully.

I reviewed all my rules for cutting wordage, and over the holidays I squeezed lifeblood out of that story in four rewrites. Each night I would count up the words I had eliminated that day. At first they were hundreds. Then they dwindled to tens. It grew progressively more painful. At the last I was pulling out single words and phrases that shrieked like mandrakes. But I told myself that it was the little man's pain, not mine, and he could learn only by suffering. With rules like razors I vivisected him unmercifully, cut the manuscript exactly in half, and sent it off again.

The little man should have hated me for it, but he did not. The day after his ordeal ended he handed up to me complete in one session a new story of only 3,500 words, shorter by half than anything I had done before. To this day I wonder whether he

was not drawing in it a portrait of himself. The opening line read: "You can't just die; you got to do it by the book," and it was the little man speaking, all right.

That story, entitled "Casey Agonistes," sold at once and became my first published work. In his letter of acceptance the editor called it "admirably terse," and I could feel the little man glow when we read that. The editor went on to ask that the story be expanded by several hundred words. I felt the little man glower. We expanded it by about fifty words and begrudged every one of them.

"Casey Agonistes" moved me from amateur to professional. The distinction is hard to define. Its salient characteristic, to me at that time and in my own terms, was that the little man had finally grasped the *idea* of learning. He began learning of his own volition. I found I could no longer read a short story purely for entertainment even if I wished to. I would note the technique as I went along, and it seemed an added dimension to the entertainment. I wonder now whether editors do not develop an intuition that tells them when a writer has crossed that invisible line and become professional. Only then, when it can be used effectively, do they offer help. In any case, 1958 became for me a year of rapid unfolding.

The story I had cut in half also sold. I began selling stories regularly. Editors would ask for revisions, and I would make them and learn by doing so. A literary agent named Rogers Terrill heard about me and "Casey" at a cocktail party and remarked casually, "Sounds like that guy might have a book in him." A mutual friend brought us together in correspondence. Terrill did not want to handle science fiction. He made a deal between us contingent upon my writing a sample straight fiction short story from which he could judge my potentiality. I set the little man searching for a suitable story idea.

Also through "Casey" I was invited to the annual science fiction writers' conference in June at Milford, Pennsylvania. It is restricted to professionals. I accepted and was hard put to get my

sample short story written and off to Rogers Terrill beforehand. I was to meet him in New York after the conference for an interview. All through those days I lived in a sense of portent. My wife went to Milford with me, and all night on the bus we did not sleep a wink.

At Milford I met writers who for years had been only names to me. They treated me as another professional, without the slightest condescension. I wish I had time today to describe Milford more fully. The writers work in isolation during the year and come from many states to gather at Milford in June. It is something like a trappers' rendezvous in the old fur-trading days. Magazine and book editors attend; sales are made, book contracts talked about, another year's work planned. The work is strangely compounded of carnival and hardheaded practicality. The latter is the tone of the workshop, which takes up most of each day, and which had the greatest influence on me.

No one can be present in the workshop but the writers themselves, and each must have one or more stories in the pool. The stories are usually ones written during the year which would not sell but which the writers are reluctant to scrap. For each, it seemed to me, the problem was how to suit the story to the mass market without sacrifice of artistic integrity. And here were men and women who wrote for a precarious living at a few cents a word, who could see both requirements clearly without setting one above the other, and who were working out a solution with all the resources of their pooled experience. I was very proud to be one of them. There was a rapport-quality to it. I felt distinctly upon me that "writing mood" which I had never before been able to attain in the presence of another human being.

We came down to New York in a daze. My wife walked with me to the interview with Rogers Terrill. She was going to leave me at the door. As a sailor I had known New York quite well, but now as we walked along it looked different. It *loomed* all around me, heavy with portent. As always, nameless people thronged along endlessly in both directions. Now they all had faces, strange

faces. Now they were the people for whom I wished to write. As we approached the busiest corner, with a shock of pleased surprise I saw a familiar face. It was Dr. Bill Poteat, in whose philosophy classes at Chapel Hill I had probed more directly into the secret of existence than perhaps in any others. We talked for only a moment, but I went along strangely reassured, as if I had been granted a favorable omen.

I talked a long while with Rogers Terrill. He was a small man with a seamed face that could crinkle into a warmly infectious smile. He said he could sell my short story if I would revise it, and he asked me if I had any plans to write a novel. I said no, that I wanted to learn as much as I could by doing short stories before I thought about novels. He agreed, and I was encouraged to tell him the thought that had crystallized in me during those workshop sessions at Milford. I said I wanted to combine literary excellence with popular appeal, without sacrifice of either, no matter how relatively unproductive I might be of marketable manuscripts. Terrill jumped up and came smiling around his desk and we shook hands on that. The handshake was our contract.

I came home to Chapel Hill feeling that I had been through something very conclusive. I found that I could get more quickly into the writing mood each morning. It was much less vulnerable to distractions. Then I began hitting a new kind of block. I would start a short story, and it would go well the first day and less well on each succeeding day until the words would stop altogether. The mood would be strongly on me and yet the words would not come. When I tried to write just anything, in order to bull through a first draft, my handwriting would go all awry. It would become large and awkward and trembly, as if I were writing with my left hand. The first time that happened I was frightened, and I stopped work for that day.

Quite soon I discovered that if I would only start writing the story over from the beginning, my hand would be free and the words would come smoothly again. I would have to start a short

story seven or eight times, each time getting a little further along with it, before I had a first draft. In terms of the game I was playing, it meant that something not apparent to me consciously went wrong with those stories along the way. The little man knew what was wrong, and the only way he could remedy it was to force a new start. With each new start there were changes, and sometimes, but not always, I thought I could see a reason for them. It made me feel floating and helpless, and I would figuratively hold my breath until I had a complete first draft. Then, however, I would have it nailed down. I could rewrite straight through as often as I wished and with more confidence than I had ever had.

The sample short story I had written for Rog Terrill was based on a yarn I had heard in China as a boy. My story did not quite reach to that yarn, but it set the stage for it. So I wrote a second story with the same characters and setting, and again I fell short of the germinal yarn. Rog sold both stories, after I had made extensive revisions, but he began telling me that I really had a novel in that material. He urged me to write it. I was reluctant to take the plunge.

However, I developed a great urge to read books on China, any book on China. The dryest book on China would hold my interest. I said that I was going to mine that material for short stories. I wrote them and Rog sold them, but in every letter he nudged me toward a novel. He said that with a few sample chapters and a synopsis he could get me a book contract. Thus I could be assured of publication before making the full investment of time and energy. By the end of 1958 he had persuaded me.

By June of 1959, in close consultation with Rog, I had written Part I of the novel at least six times. It ran well over a hundred pages. Rog arranged for some quick readings while I attended my second Milford conference. I had moved clear out of science fiction and into the men's magazines, but they still welcomed me at Milford. I went down to New York and spent a week reading files of old Chinese newspapers in the Public Library while Rog angled for a book contract. He tried three publishers and failed.

Then he said I would have to rewrite. We talked over how I would do it, in the light of the editorial reactions.

Home in Chapel Hill, I seemed to lack the heart to go on with it. Probably in an effort to escape, and with a kind of false and feverish zeal, I explored the Spanish-American War, oil tankers, and early nineteenth-century pirates. Nothing I wrote was much good. Sometime about September I developed an urge to read Hemingway. I considered such capricious urges to be signals from the little man. For some reason he wanted to read Hemingway.

We had studied Hemingway before, but this was different. We stopped writing and read everything of Hemingway in print in a state of sustained, nonanalytical excitement. We came out of it with the concept of the "clean, well-lighted story." I will not try to explain it. It is the little man's concept, a matter of pure feeling, and the most he can do is grimace and point to "Big Two-hearted River." The experience had the feeling of a change in kind, as with "Casey Agonistes." Thereafter, in a manner impossible to convey, I wrote from a different posture, with a kind of spiritual body-English unknown to me until then. The first story I wrote from that posture, and very clumsily, sold to the *Saturday Evening Post*.

In the fall of that year, 1959, I had a chance to buy the house I now live in on Cobb Terrace. I bought it with misgivings. The down payment took the last of my Navy savings, and I was fearful of what economic insecurity might do to my writing. I would no longer be able to rent the office. But the house had an extra room which I could hedge about with the same tabus as my office, and I gambled that my work habits had become dependable enough to stand the transfer. The last story I wrote in my office was the *Post* sale, and it furnished our new kitchen.

The *Post* sale eased my feelings of insecurity. I decided that I would stay on short stories until the house was paid for and I had a small cash reserve again, before starting the long pull on

the novel. For the next several years I was going to write primarily for money.

I stopped reading about China. I studied scores of *Post* stories, and I tailored every line I wrote specifically for the *Post*—and the *Post* would not buy any more stories. They always found something wrong with them too vague to remedy. When Rog tried them at other slick magazines the editors would say: "This is so obviously a *Post* story that I wonder you haven't given it to them." Rog told me it was just a symptom of what was happening to the magazine market and the reason he was urging all his clients who could do so to shift to novels. He wanted me to take up the China novel again.

I still held back. I gave up on the *Post* and tried stories for the men's magazines and even science fiction again. There was more desperation than pleasure in the work. By July, nine months had passed and I had made only one small sale. I realized I might just as well have been working on the novel all that while. With a sudden and angry resolution, I burned my bridges. I went back to the novel with a vow as solemn as marriage that I would write it through to the end. I did not care whether I had a book contract or how many years it took.

At once the work went well and smoothly. My thirst for China reading came back redoubled. I rewrote Part I several times and sent it to Rog just before Christmas. I had built up a kind of momentum, and I went right on with Part II while I was waiting to hear from Rog. Very soon I began to get the signal that the little man wanted to start over again, but with Part II. A feeling grew in me that the novel properly started with Part II. Late in January, with a curious kind of relief, I heard from Rog that Part I and my synopsis had again been rejected. I wrote Rog that I was scrapping Part I and that I was going to take the novel through a complete draft before I again showed anything to anyone. The next day I started afresh on Part II with the sense that I was at last really beginning a novel.

Thus began for me still another phase. My life began to contract wholly into my work. I became increasingly reluctant to go
out evenings. I wanted the time for reading. But I could read
nothing that did not, in some way not always known to me, relate
to my work. When I tried to read simply for pleasure, I could
not. Several times I hurled a book across the room and was
astonished at myself afterward. I gave up reading newspapers on
the plea to myself that I would keep up with the world by reading *Time* magazine every week. Then every Wednesday, when
Time came blundering in like a Person from Porlock, I grew to
hate the sight of it. Once I could not have imagined myself not
reading the *Scientific American* avidly on its day of arrival, but
now I was letting months of it pile up unread. Yet all the while I
was reading voraciously, with the feeling that the demands of
society would not let me read nearly as much as I needed.

My choice of reading was very whimsical. Sometimes I would
read just the beginnings of novels and sometimes just the end-
ings. For one stretch I read China novels and for another stretch
I read dozens of military novels. I read a lot in the social sciences.
All the while I read all the nonfiction China books I could find.
When I did not know what I wanted to read next, I learned to go
along the shelves of my library and leaf into books at random
until one would engage my interest. When it did, I could almost
feel the gears click into place. The cutoff would be equally
abrupt. One night *Middlemarch* clicked into place for me and an
hour later clicked off. I don't know what I wanted of it.

That was how it went for me. I wrote seven days a week and
read every evening that I could. I became almost completely secluded. I would not answer letters. I let them pile up for months
and then, resentfully, I would take a day off and answer them all
at once. June neared, and I wrote to my friends at Milford that
I could not come that year. I was afraid that if I broke my stride
even for a few days I would not be able to pick it up again. As I
neared the end of the first draft in July, a kind of superstitious
terror grew in me, a haunting fear that some malignity of fate

would stop me short. But nothing did, and I completed the first draft. I knew I had the novel nailed down.

Without loss of a day I began a second draft. In September I sent eight chapters and a synopsis up to Rog. I went right on working. In November Rog phoned me that Harper & Brothers were going to give me a contract for it. The news thrilled me and brought a tremendous exultation. I could not work any more that day. Nothing since has quite touched again the glory of that afternoon. After that, if possible, I worked with even more drive. The first half of the advance reached me just before Christmas. For my wife and me that was the happiest Christmas since our marriage six years before. On Christmas Day I wrote three thousand words.

In February I finished the second draft and went up to New York to confer with my editor, Marion S. Wyeth, Jr., on revisions. Rog joined us, and we talked through a long afternoon in a rapport very like that of the workshop at Milford. I came home and worked on revisions at the same pace. I kept in close touch with Rog and with Buz Wyeth, and our working rapport intensified. I no longer had the sense of being alone at my desk. It was a genuine group mind that worked out the final form of *Sand Pebbles*. Although I wrote all the words, I know I could not possibly have taken the novel to finished form in isolation.

A few days before June I finished the work. Milford for my wife and me that year was almost all carnival.

The story of my development as a writer properly ends here. For almost a year now I have not written anything of large scope. But I will recount briefly what has happened during the past year, because it is part of the larger story of my life in Chapel Hill.

Through July and August I worked up a quite detailed plot outline for another novel. In August the good news began, first the book club sale and then magazine serialization. In September I went to New York for the *Times* interview that was to break the story of the Harper Prize. While I was in New York the movie

sale went through. And Rog went to the hospital with a heart attack and pulmonary complications.

I had brought the plot outline of the new novel with me to New York. Rog and Buz and I talked it over. From his hospital bed Rog negotiated a contract for it without a word of it yet written. I promised Rog that I would go right to work writing it. I said that when I came up in January for the publication of *Sand Pebbles* I would bring him one chapter of the new novel as a token.

I did not write a word of it. My correspondence had increased very greatly, and I seemed to spend much of each day answering letters. Rog came out of the hospital, but my health faltered and I went in for several weeks. I had still not fully recovered when I had to go back to New York in January. How I survived those three weeks in New York still amazes me. I promised Rog that I would bring him three chapters when I came up in February. Then I escaped home to Chapel Hill as if to a sanctuary.

It was no longer a sanctuary. I had a mountain of accumulated correspondence. I had to write speeches for delivery in Washington and New York. When I reached New York again in mid-February, I did not have even one chapter of the new novel. Through all that stay Rog chided me gently about my delay in getting back to my own proper work. He warned me at length of the difficulty of writing a second novel when the first has scored heavily. On my last night in New York we and our wives went out to dinner together, and all evening he kept on that theme. When we said goodbye, I slapped him on the shoulder and told him: "Rog, for sure now, I'm going home and go to work. We're going to do it again."

In Chapel Hill two days later I learned of his sudden death.

That brings my story up to date. Since last June I have not developed at all as a writer, although I have gained some competence at being a public figure of sorts. There is something frighteningly seductive about it. In another month I will have been idle for a full year, and I hardly know where the time has gone.

So for my own salvation as a writer I am going once again to burn my ships on the coast of Mexico. I have set June 1 as an absolute cut-off date for all engagements which will work to delay or distract me from going to work full time on the new novel.

Let me in conclusion summarize what up to this point I think I have learned about professional writing. What I will say is not necessarily valid for anyone other than myself. And I speak from out the dust of continuing battle, so I may interpret my experience somewhat differently ten years from now. But here is how it seems to me today.

Learning creative writing is a process of training the unconscious. We all have in us a living something independent of that which thinks it says "I" for the whole man. It is not enough to know it intellectually; one must also learn it through lived experience, which is a quite different way of knowing. What I did was to grant it a separate "I," to personify it as "the little man." I reached out my hand to him, and we clasped hands, to give help and to receive help.

At first the little man can learn only by doing, by blind trial and corrected error. It may take him years to learn on his level what the conscious mind can learn in a month of hard study. But the creative quality of what is written cannot improve any faster than the little man can learn. For that little man is the powerhouse of all creative writing.

He it is who explores the caverns measureless to man and therein listens to ancestral voices. He is the sole author, the scenarist, and all of the actors in our private dreams. His original media are visual imagery and feeling tones and only a few spoken words. Until a few years ago, my little man was illiterate. Sometimes printed matter would appear in my dreams, and when I tried to focus down and read it he would snatch it away. When I gained enough power over him to hold it in place, the presumed letters would turn out to be blurs and squiggles. There was great tension in the dream at such moments. But the time came when the letters were genuine and did not dissolve.

My theory for the moment is that the little man must learn how to change himself from a private to a public dreamer. He must learn how to transmute his original media into words in such a way that the story will induce in readers something resembling the unconscious, nonverbal complex of imagery and feeling tones he began with. The professionally written story may be a kind of collective and public dream. From the start, my little man tried hard. I found my unsalable first stories so deeply satisfying that it was very painful to cut and revise. I wanted just to reread them and glow with pleasure. In that phase the dreams were fully verbalized but still private. To make them collective and public demanded a subtle but equally as radical a change in verbal structuring as mirror drawing demands in hand-eye coordination. Now I take professional pride and find considerable pleasure in rewriting. I have little pleasure in reading the published work.

For me I think the preliminary movement was best and soonest made in painful isolation. Perhaps there had to be pain, to make the little man start learning. Along the way that I was going solicitous critical help too early might have been a hindrance; at least I felt it so. So would have been premature publication in any subsidized or coterie outlet. Both would have seemed to me a kind of substitute gratification, whereas the gratification I sought lay in breaking through to Everyman in the dust and heat of the common marketplace.

For me the breakthrough came in two critical junctures. I think with "Casey Agonistes" the little man first grasped the principle of public dreaming and thereafter set himself to learn and apply it more fully. I believe, however, that he still thought he was the only little man in the universe and that he was still working for the familiar single spectator, who had suddenly grown outrageously demanding. Not until well over a year later did he learn from Hemingway that the theater was really public and all the seats were filled with other little men just like himself.

That, I think, was the source of the strange excitement with

which he and I read Hemingway that time. My little man was learning that he was not alone. The clean, well-lighted story has in it a quality of deep calling to deep which will not yield to critical analysis. It can never be imposed upon or demanded of the little man by the intellect. It is the treasure that he must alone and voluntarily bring up from the deep waters. When he can bring it safely to shore, he breaks free of the solitary confinement into which the evolving human condition has plunged all the little men. Momentarily he can permit the other little men to feel that they are not alone either.

They say Leonardo was ambidextrous from infancy and could write in mirror-reversal without ever having had to practice it. Maybe he painted Mona Lisa in some looking-glass way that makes her a universal public dream-image. Possibly Leonardo remained a whole man from birth. I know that I did not. But more and more I find the little man and myself tending to co-exist in the same "I." Perhaps the measure of artistic maturity is the degree of that coexistence and the calm joy it brings is the true reward of writing.